D1177776

From the Author of *Letters from Tony*

BEYOND
SUNDAY
MORNING

Stories and Perspectives for Integrating Faith and Life

From the Author of *Letters from Tony*

BEYOND
SUNDAY
MORNING

Stories and Perspectives for Integrating Faith and Life

TONY CARVALHO

Beyond Sunday Morning is a collection of wonderfully written essays that provide a path to spiritual enlightenment. Each essay will help you take a step forward in your faith and inspire you to run after Christ. Tony Carvalho is an incredible writer, storyteller, and apologist—not to mention an outstanding Christian Servant Leader. If you are desiring to better understand the goodness of God, look no further. Your heart will be encouraged and your soul will be fed "Beyond Sunday Morning"!
DR. ADAM WRIGHT: President of Dallas Baptist University, Dallas, Texas

After reading this book I did something I never imagined I would do. I started a Bible study at work. Tony has a gifted way of hitting you over the head with the truth, without hitting you over the head. This is a timely wake-up call and reminder that Jesus comes first, no matter what. No matter where you are, no matter what you believe, this is a valuable book that our world needs right now. Clever, witty, thought-provoking, and inspiring. This is one that I will read over and over again, and I've already read it three times.
BROOKE WARD: Ward Timber, Ltd., Linden, Texas

Tony's target audience is typically young, educated, intelligent individuals who aren't satisfied with conclusions drawn from philosophy class, contemporary culture or traditional church. They want more info to solve questions that may or may not have already been answered from their perspective. Some don't believe in God at all. Some do, but aren't sure if they can trust him or God's Word. Some are dedicated followers of Jesus who just want to be prepared to have an answer for everyone they encounter.
AARON SUTTON: Graphic Designer, Pure White Design, Santa Rosa Beach, Florida

Practical, concise, and rooted in Scripture. These are the words that come to my mind as I read Tony's book, *Beyond Sunday Morning*. Tony has a way of packing a punch within these brief chapters while, at the same time, driving you to truly contemplate the point he is making within each one. This is a book that will challenge the average congregant within the church to truly consider the difference Christ is making within their lives and within the workplace God has them in. Everyone can benefit from *Beyond Sunday Morning*.
DANIEL GARNETT: U.S. Army Chaplain

As a Christian university administrator, it has been my life's work to integrate faith and learning to equip students to be Christian servant leaders in their respective callings. In this book a dear friend of mine, Tony Carvalho, does not just integrate faith and learning, but rather he aids Christians in going beyond that into our central calling of integrating faith and living. *Beyond Sunday Morning* is a wonderful guide from a gifted business leader who has implemented these practices into his own life and work. This book is insightful, challenging, and inspiring.
DR. GARY COOK: Chancellor of Dallas Baptist University, Dallas, Texas

Does the author love the Scriptures? Yes. Does he love God? It goes without saying. It appears Mr. Carvalho's objective is to prepare a work wherein "believers" are unapologetic about "the faith" and eagerly and knowledgably share it with others.
REVEREND CLAUDE FILLINGIM: Hutchinson, Kansas

Beyond Sunday Morning gives a unique perspective on many often-asked questions of the Christian faith. In a series of short essays, Tony Carvalho addresses these questions with the grace and skill of a gifted teacher, giving the reader just enough information to excite further study. If you are looking for a fun yet though-provoking read, I recommend *Beyond Sunday Morning*. It provides the spiritual lift many of us can use periodically.
ANTHONY ALEXANDER: President, Extended Borders International Ministries

Beyond Sunday Morning is thoughtful, insightful, and personal! Tony's stories and perspectives will motivate you to think of God's story in your own personal life!
FELIX RODRIGUEZ: Physical Education Teacher, Plano, Texas

Tony Carvalho writes with a personal wit mixed with a passion for Jesus. It's obvious he longs for fellow Christ-followers to get serious about the Lord and for those yet to believe to know the truth claims of Jesus. Tony's intelligence and practical theology make for an easy but challenging read. Get your copy and share it.
DR. GARY WIGGINS: Seagrove Baptist Church, Santa Rosa Beach, Florida

Beyond Sunday Morning:
Stories and Perspectives for Integrating Faith and Life
Tony Carvalho

978-1-7337785-3-4: (Kindle)
978-1-7337785-4-1: (Hardcover Print)
978-1-7337785-5-8: (Audio)

Lead Editor: Benjamin Jones
Assistant Editor: Ryan Thompson

Scripture quotations taken from the New International Version (NIV), Holy Bible, New International Version®, NIV® Copyright ©1973, 1978, 1984, 2011 by Biblica, Inc.® Used by permission. All rights reserved worldwide.

Cover illustration "Porch Time with Abbey" by Lauren Pingree. Cover by Aaron Sutton, founder of Pure White Design.

Acknowledgements

· · · · · · · · · · · · · · · · · · ·

I want to thank Ben Jones, my lead editor. He is a relatively recent graduate from one of my favorite places on earth, Dallas Baptist University. Without his patience, recommendations and excellent work, you would not be reading this book. He glued together all the broken pieces I sent his way for well over a year. I only stumped him once. Pilot error on my part. Apparently, he wasn't aware that some fossils still around today, could still refer to a television as a tube.

And of course, as long as I am rowing this boat, I must recognize R.C. Sproul at Ligonier as the one who ignited my passion and desire to pursue truth, rational thought and apologetics. Wait. Did I just confess to being irrational before reading Sproul?

Dr. Jesse Nelson, my dear friend in Panama City (Florida not Central America), is primarily the one responsible for my transition from talking to writing. Don't like the book? Blame him. You can contact him at the following email address: thenexttonyevans@gmail.com Actually, no you can't, but yes, he possibly is.

To my immediate family: Tony and Emily and Carmen, Jennifer and Se Yoon, Lauren and Steve, with all their dogs and cats, you are my heaven on earth. For all those who either dribbled in or deluged me with feedback during the writing of the manuscript, thank you, sincerely. To friends and relatives, and just people I bumped into along the journey, their encouragement to keep it simple, and to not negotiate the basic truths of the faith, kept me centered.

To my new friends and ministry partners Carl Dobrowolski, Bill Giarratana, Frank Gomez, and Jim Holmes of Goodwill Rights Management Corp. I can rightfully point to them, for not only recommending we put together Lehigh Ministries Media, but for "making it so." Great idea guys. Kudos (from the Greek of course) to you all.

And a special thank you to the Bible Study frequent-ladies and seldom-men at Chief Oil & Gas, who spent many hours with me for a decade. Literally. We studied and prayed, laughed and laughed some more, enjoying the time we spent getting to know our Lord Jesus Christ better and better as the years marched on. And of course, without Him leading the way, not one of us could ever accomplish anything worth doing. *Give thanks to the* LORD, *for he is good; his love endures forever* (Psalm 118:1).

To Diane,
As time goes on
I realize
Chicago 1970

Foreword

In 1947 the "Doomsday Clock" was invented as a symbolic representation of how close humanity is to creating and causing a man-made catastrophic event leading to the destruction of the world. At the time of my writing, the Doomsday Clock is the closest it has ever been to midnight since its creation. Aren't you glad you decided to read the foreword?!

The world seems to be at an inflection point. Everywhere we turn we are reminded of current events that point toward a global destabilization unlike any other time in human history. Yet, in reality, we tend to have a short-term memory and fail to realize there have been much worse recorded times in human history than what we experience today.

Even in the midst of declining financial markets, threats of another looming and more serious global pandemic than what we lived through with COVID-19, social, racial, and cultural woes, not to mention wars and rumors of wars, we are far better off as a human race than we have ever been. The global absolute poverty rate has fallen from just more than 40% to under 10% in recent years, natural resources have become cheaper and more abundant, and the average life expectancy has more than doubled since 1900, reaching more than 72 years. So there is indeed some positive news amidst a world steeped in negativity.

Yes, it is true, that the world is in a mess – and life as we know it these past few years has collectively driven the world to higher levels of anxiety, depression, suicide, substance abuse, and a mood of pessimism unlike we have known. And I get the sense, that for many, we have arrived at a near breaking point. I recently shared with a group that we are a people running on empty attempting to minister to a people on empty.

If you have had more sleepless nights than you can recall in recent days, or you find yourself caught up in a mind maze of worry, fear, anxiety, or deep unsettling, then I have hopeful news for you. There is a cure.

The promises discovered in God's Word are just as true today as they were when originally written. Please, don't stop reading now. There is an important message to be heard. Let me challenge you with something. Just as Paul admonished us in Philippians 4, think on things that are true, honest, just, pure, lovely, good, and praiseworthy. Guard your heart and mind and then experience what follows. The peace of Christ.

After having served in Christian higher education for more than two decades now, working with countless leaders at all levels of leadership, both in and out of the university setting, I am convinced more than ever of the power of God's Word discovered in the Bible. I have discovered a deeper personal meaning for life, as well as a hope and faith that every solution to every problem ever encountered is discovered right there in the Bible. The problem is, few will ever give the actual time necessary to go to this incredible instruction manual and become enlightened on how to truly live the good life.

While I am increasingly hopeful by a generation of Christian leaders and emerging scholars filling our classrooms at DBU, I am equally shocked by the amount of biblical illiteracy plaguing our young people today. And for the most part, these are students that grew up in Christian homes, going to church on most Sundays!

As I do my work at DBU, I hold very sacred our vision and mission as a nationally ranked, comprehensive, liberal arts university, to build a great university that is pleasing to God, integrate faith and learning, and produce servant leaders that will transform the world. I stress many times over to our students that every single one of us has a special purpose in this life. A unique story to tell. But the best road map in discovering God's way for living, is sadly often ignored, disregarded, or diminished as outdated, irrelevant, and too traditional.

If you are reading this, there is breath in your lungs, more life to live, a testimony to give, and heart to encourage and one to be encouraged.

Typically, in life, I have found that we are either living in a storm, coming out of one, or preparing to go in one. Another way a mentor in my life put it, we are constantly living a series of blessings and battles every day. One of the distinctives of the life we have been given is the personal growth realized by living through these storms and the encouragement we have to offer others through shared experiences.

What my good friend, Tony Carvalho, has done in this inspirational book is show us Jesus in a fresh way through his story. He demonstrates in a winsome way how anyone can captain a ship in calm waters, but how incredible Christian leadership is forged by navigating stormy seas through crucible moments. Tony helps us discover the deep meaning of walking by faith and not by sight, trusting that God's way is always safer than a known way.

The iconic philosopher, Francis Bacon, is attributed to have remarked that, "some books are to be tasted, others are to be swallowed, and some few to be chewed and digested." What you have in your hands is worth feasting on.

My buddy, Tony, has been to the mountain tops and walked through valleys and has lived to give a very special gift in sharing his story. Through it all, he has shown us how to live a life that is daily dependent on God and being redeemed for a purpose beyond what he can even begin to realize this side of heaven. If you let it, Tony's story will change and challenge you. It did me. And that's what is fun about how our amazing God works. He uses broken vessels like you and me to tell what we think is our story, but in reality, it's His story, and providentially woven together in a way that creates a beautiful tapestry, creating a good thing for His glory.

Many years ago a good friend of mine gave me the book, "Valley of Vision," a collection of Puritan prayers that have shaped my faith and formation. As I experience what Tony has allowed the Lord to use him to do, I am reminded of the Valley of Vision Prayer, as illustrated by the many stories you will read in this book. I too, believe that if each of us reflects deeply enough, through the depths of life we have lived, "we will see thee in the heights."

The Valley of Vision

· · · · · · · · · · · · · · · · ·

Thou hast brought me to the valley of vision,
Where I live in the depths but see thee in the heights;
Hemmed in by mountains of sin I behold thy glory.

Let me learn by paradox
That the way down is the way up,
that to be low is to be high,
that the broken heart is the healed heart,
that the contrite spirit is the rejoicing spirit,
that the repenting soul is the victorious soul,
that to have nothing is to possess all,
that to bear the cross is to wear the crown,
that to give is to receive,
that the valley is the place of vision.

Adam C. Wright, Ph.D.
President, Dallas Baptist University

Preface

The *Stories and Perspectives* that I present here are mere morsels, teasers that can perhaps be thought of as early investigations for those searching for a greater understanding of the Christian faith. My purpose is to simply ignite, in an uncompromising and unnegotiable yet fun way, a desire to dive deeper. Bible studies should be fun, and the pursuit of our faith should generate excitement. Unravelling the greatest mysteries, answering the most important and demanding questions, grappling with the most taxing obstacles—if handled properly and successfully—can be the thrill of a lifetime.

I am a lay person with no degrees or work experience within the field. In this regard, the closest I come to building a resume prior to writing a book would be my experience in leading a Bible Study at my last job. People have asked and continue to ask me occasionally what I did or what my position was when I was working. Assuming they are in search of a business-card title, I could have used a keyword, such as Senior Vice President, but there were times when I would gladly reply, "I led a Bible Study." Depending on the individual and/or circumstance, responses landed easily in only two categories. First, "That's great! I wish we had a Bible Study at work." My volley back was automatic, having returned the slow serve numerous times. "Why don't you?" The other broad category did not generate many words but rather an obviously stunned character and perspiration. I assumed the unspoken reply was "How could anybody mention the word Bible in public? Show me the exit!"

This experience was only partly foundational to my desire to continue doing some kind of ministry work in retirement, but, honestly, I never seriously thought I would write a couple of books. By the way, the Bible mentions retirement only once in the book of Numbers 8:25. This verse very specifically pertains to the Levitical priesthood. I assume Aaron negotiated—on behalf of TULIP (the Trade Union of the Levitical Israeli Priesthood) and three-thousand years before John Calvin—one heck of an agreement to make it possible for the Israelites to hit the beach at the age of fifty. But the rest of us should willingly sprint to the finish line. Every Christian is in full-time ministry, whether we know it or not. The idea of writing was planted by a close friend—a pastor from a local church—who very recently finished a doctorate at an internationally recognized Seminary. Logic 101 suggested it: if this made sense to him with his credentials, it should make sense to me.

The other thing that motivated me into writing *Beyond Sunday Morning* was the simple fact that we have become so overwhelmed in nearly every way. We are drowning. Overloaded. Is this really necessary? No. But that won't change anytime soon. So, the decision was made to take an important topic and purposefully boil it down into easily digestible pieces. People love short stories for a lot of reasons, but one is simply that we no longer seem to have the time or ability to focus on the entire volume. Rather than fight city hall, I folded like a cheap novel (pun intended) and set out to write down short stories—mere suggestions to generate thought and a commitment to fight this natural curse. Will the readers often say, "Tony, I never thought of that?" Maybe or maybe not. How about, "Tony, I never really understood that topic, but now it is starting to make sense to me"? Perhaps. If I can generate excitement and a desire to pursue the things that really matter and, at least for a few moments, ignore the television, emails, Internet, and social media, I have accomplished my goal.

Have fun with *Beyond Sunday Morning*, and, as always, when you make it to the last page, please consider getting in touch with me through the Lehigh Ministries website. I would love to hear from you. Also, please consider handing off the book to a friend or relative who might benefit from a glimpse at the questions, and possible answers, they may often contemplate.

Introduction

Yes, I wrote this last. Partly because that is what you are supposed to do, and partly because I had no idea what I was going to say. The sixty-five-plus-one essays came "naturally." Arranging, ordering, or, if I may sound like a nerd, categorizing the essays was indeed challenging. And to this moment I can only tell you that I did my best to stack the essays in an order that will be helpful to you, dear reader. I actually contemplated writing each title on a 3x5 card (*a what?*) and having a kid come over to pick them up after I tossed them on the living room floor. Maybe that wasn't the best way to do it, so I gave it a bit more thought.

I really wanted to start with the fun stuff. I *really* wanted to. But thought, followed by prayer (backwards again), told me not to. This being backed up by a pastor and friend who has better insight than I do, the decision was made to start with the drier component. I hesitate to call it the not-so-much-fun part because I find (as I hope you do or will) this stuff is incredibly fun and fascinating. Apologetics—arguing for the faith or defending the faith with reason—gets a bad rap sometimes. This may be because it is perceived by many to be dry, theological, or intellectual. And what difference does it make anyway? Short answer? All the difference in the world!

So, rather than tossing titles, I decided to arrange the articles into four categories. When you make it to the last page, you may very well wonder why (and continue to wonder why) I did it that way. I started with what we believe, from a Conservative Biblical Christian (CBC) perspective. We must start here, or what follows could be misinterpreted—a misfire in the making. I have some light and entertaining stuff packed into the rest of this book, but entertaining wasn't my primary goal. And let's face it: The overwhelming majority of spiritual stuff in this world could never be put into the CBC category. Apparently, someone counted up four-thousand-five-hundred religions existing in the world today. I am only interested in one.

The first part, *Challenges to the Christian Faith*, is just that—a dozen essays written to set the stage and whet your appetite for more. Volumes have been written in this category. I believe I touched on nearly all the major criticisms to our faith.

The second part, *Putting the Bible First, Sola Scriptura*, is a bit of a smorgasbord (but just wait until parts three and four). Here I talk about the Bible, sometimes in a backdoor way, taking a different approach. I ask, "Where Are the Funny Stories in the Bible?" and "Why Are We Compared to Sheep?" keeping it light. But then I follow up with "The Scariest Chapter in the Bible" and "Total Recall," which will take some getting used to. One of my favorite essays in this part, and I hope yours too, is "Ask the Author," where I purposefully don't tell the whole story.

The third part, *Putting Yourself in Scoring Position*, is where you may get a jolt. Yes, newsflash—God is alive and well and answers prayers with very straightforward and fun, yes *fun*, responses and situations. In essays like "Billboards" and "Pizzas," the real fun begins. But this is where I continue with the practical comments such as how can we attack the divorce rate in the church, how can we start each day in the Lord's presence, and let's start thinking about big things—the fantastic things—that God is waiting for *all* of us to pursue.

The fourth part, *Winning Each Day No Matter the Score*, a continuation of part three, is simply my thoughts to further integrate faith and life. Sounds great, now—but how do we do it? Wait. *Should* we do it? We have to cross that bridge first. Some humor embedded, of course, but let's fight it out. We live in a culture that in some ways is in free fall. I am waiting for the next book to really light the fire. For now, when you turn on the TV, when you deal with the "neighbors," what is really going on? Try "Running Away from Falsehood and Lies" and "You Are What You Eat." Come up for air if need be with "Anybody Have a Bible Handy?"

Have fun. As I mentioned earlier, please, let me know how I did. More importantly, how did you do? Life isn't this hard. We make it hard. Winning each day, no matter the score, is possible only if we put on our personal-Christian-worldview spectacles and *never* take them off.

PART ONE:

Challenges to the Christian Faith

How Do I Know
the Bible is True?

"You are required to believe, to preach, and to teach what
the Bible says is true, not what you want the Bible to say is
true."
—R.C. Sproul[1]

"If your creed and Scripture do not agree, cut your creed to
pieces, but make it agree with this book. If there be anything
in the church to which you belong which is contrary to the
inspired Word, leave that church."
—Charles Spurgeon[2]

It is true that we can know a fair amount about God by looking
out the window, walking through the world discovering
who He is, understanding something of His character by
contemplating the beauty and complexity of the natural world.
We call this *General Revelation.*

In Romans 1:20 Paul states, "For since the creation of the world
God's invisible qualities—his eternal power and divine nature—
have been clearly seen, being understood from what has been
made, so that people are without excuse." And Psalm 19:1-2 reads,
"The heavens declare the glory of God; the skies proclaim the
work of his hands. Day after day they pour forth speech; night
after night they reveal knowledge."

But we are interested in so much more. We want to know as
much about God as possible, and that means hearing His voice,
finding all sources of special revelation, and delving deeper

---

1   Sproul, R.C. [@RCSproul]. (2016, January 29). [Tweet]. Twitter. https://twitter.
com/rcsproul/status/693171658287378432?lang=en

2   Spurgeon, C. (1988). *Spurgeon at his best: Over 2200 striking quotations from
the world's most exhaustive and widely-read sermon series* (T. Carter, Ed.). Baker
Book House.

and deeper into Scripture. Since everything we as Christians believe as authoritative comes from Scripture (sola Scriptura or Scripture alone), I found it necessary to jump in, even if only with one foot rather than two. Dear reader, after taking a look at the Boiled Down Carvalho (BDC) notes below, please take this opportunity—regardless of whether or not you are totally convinced of the inerrancy, authority, and uniqueness of Scripture— to pursue a study of your own on this subject. Nothing is more important. I have written elsewhere on the primary pursuit—epistemology—which is the study of knowledge: How do we know, or how can we determine truth? We will not get very far in our understanding of the Christian faith until we are convinced, beyond a shadow of a doubt, that the current-day translations are accurate. Google the term "biblical inerrancy." Wait—a better idea. Go to Amazon and order something from our friends R.C. Sproul, Josh McDowell, John MacArthur, or Norman L. Geisler. You pick one. There are plenty of excellent books available.

I quote exclusively from the New International Version (NIV) in *Letters from Tony* and this book. I still believe the NIV is the most readable. It is a thought-for-thought rendering, smooth to the ear and accurate. For a better understanding or translation of the ancient languages, students will pick up the New American Standard Bible (NASB). This translation seems a bit choppy, so many have decided to pull back slightly and they prefer the English Standard Version (ESV). The ESV is my favorite. Yes, a bit choppy still and odd to our tewnty-first-century ears, but it does an excellent job of bringing forward a word-for-word translation.

The Bible was written by forty authors over 1,500 years or 2,200 years, if you assume Job was written by Job or one of his contemporaries. Think of the settings—not only time periods but cultures, backgrounds, perspectives, languages, and influences—that the writers carried throughout their lives. Given all this significant variation, the story they tell is the same. No contradictions. Imagine trying to duplicate that today. Read or listen to more than one mass-media outlet, like television, Internet, or radio, on any given subject or event. There is often significant variation to the narrative. How can we know what really happened? Many times, we cannot.

Scripture is accurate from a historical and archaeological perspective. We must be careful to not assume that if something has not been found, it invalidates Scripture. No. It just hasn't been found.

The claim is that Scripture is inerrant in the *original* manuscript. We allow for slight copying errors. These errors, for the most part, have been discovered—all of which are not vital to the foundational doctrines. In this regard, biblical scholars believe we can claim the current day New Testament renderings are essentially 99 percent—or more—accurate. There is significant textural purity and internal consistency throughout. To further understand this concept, please consider doing an online search, using keywords such as "Dead Sea Scrolls." The Scrolls, found in 1947, provided even greater confirmation. Also consider doing a search on "The Doctrine of Preservation." It makes little sense, knowing something of the nature of God, that He would allow Man to alter His words to us. Is God truly sovereign? Why would He come into human time and space (as Immanuel) to suffer intensely on our behalf, and then allow this message of hope to be corrupted by human endeavors? How could the message of God's indescribable love for us not be communicated effectively, essentially being derailed or hijacked by a few, if not many, incompetent or evil players? He would have made certain that His word would be preserved literally forever. As one verse from the Bible reads, "The grass withers and the flowers fall, but the word of our God endures forever" (Isa. 40:8).

Translators will commonly go back to ancient manuscripts. This is not the game of telephone used earlier in school to demonstrate how truth is twisted due to repetition or the retelling of a story. With better understanding of the original languages, there is more accuracy in the most modern translations. There are about 6,000 early Greek manuscripts of the New Testament. Compare these numbers to what we have from writers such as Plato, Aristotle, Caesar, and Homer. There are fewer than 2,000 manuscripts of Homer's *Iliad*. Few of us ever wondered if Homer really meant what he said when he declared that "Life and death are balanced as it were on the edge of a razor" (*The Iliad of Homer* 10.173-174)[3]. Is that really what the Apostle Homer wrote?

We have the idea that the Bible was put together many years after the actual writings and that deciding which books would be chosen for inclusion was a prolonged and heated debate. This is not true. Almost exclusively, the writings were accepted as canonical when they were written and read. In a very rare instance, we continue to debate the authorship of Hebrews, originally thought to be another Pauline Letter.

We should recall that in early Hebrew tradition, the culture was obsessed with truth. Whether in writings or legal proceedings, precision in describing events vividly with clarity—especially when invoking God's hand—was commonly viewed as a sacred pursuit. The biblical writers believed they were speaking the very words of God. Just a few examples include: "The Lord Says," occurs 188 times in the Bible, "The Lord said to me," 37 times, "Hear the Word of the Lord," 34 times. As a sidebar note, the Bible could only have been written by good guys (human or angelic) or bad guys (human or demonic). Bad guys don't tell people to be good, and good guys would never lie about God being the author. This tongue-in-cheek quip leaves God as the sole remaining possibility.

Another interesting perspective is that the writers are so painfully honest. At times, they clearly come across as falling short (a nice way to put it). Recall Peter denying Christ, and Moses arguing with God about returning to Egypt. If Scripture was man-breathed, the writers most likely would have casually forgotten to include the parts that made them look less than gallant.

And the ultimate authority, our Lord of course, believed every word of the Old Testament. This can be shown in numerous passages, but my favorite is this one from the book of Matthew 5:17-18: "Do not think that I have come to abolish the Law or the Prophets; I have not come to abolish them but to fulfill them. For truly I tell you, until heaven and earth disappear, not the

3   Homer. 2011. *The Iliad of Homer* (S. Butler, Trans.) Bartleby.com. (Original work published ca. 800-700 BCE)

smallest letter, not the least stroke of a pen, will by any means disappear from the Law until everything is accomplished."

The best argument to advance the God-breathed claim of Scripture? Prophesies fulfilled, the future predicted—an exclusive God-thing. Jesus fulfilled over 300 prophecies. That clearly proves who Jesus was and who wrote the prophecies. Many believe that the two most striking chapters in the Old Testament that clearly depict the intense suffering of our Lord on the Cross are Psalm 22 and Isaiah 53. The narrative actually begins at the conclusion of chapter 52 in verses 12-15. No one doubts that these Old Testament passages were penned hundreds of years before the crucifixion yet read like eyewitness reports.

Can I trust the Bible? Yes. With your life.

Why Should I Have to Pay for Adam and Eve's Mistake?

"But evil has been around since the Garden of Eden, and God's plan for victory was designed before the world began. The Bible tells us to fear no evil."
—David Jeremiah[4]

"There is no time in human history when you were more perfectly represented than in the Garden of Eden."
—R. C. Sproul[5]

The ongoing chant repeated throughout the years, similar to "Unfair to Local 12," is the protest of God's treatment of His children starting from the earliest days in the Garden of Eden. God is accused of putting together a rotten deal. He creates two people, and what do they do? Blow it. All it took was a brief encounter with Satan disguised as a serpent or snake. The serpent spoke to Eve with disarming cunning and craftiness. See Genesis 3 starting in verse 1. We can describe the encounter as sinister. Satan successfully manipulated his prey, resulting in Adam and Eve's decision to disobey the Lord. Sin enters the world, and, because we are all related to our original parents, we inherit their disease. What's up with that?

The assumption (recognized or not) is that we could have done better. Logically, then, we shouldn't throw a fit if we are convinced that we also would have failed the test. So, let's take a

---

4   Jeremiah, D. (2018). *Ever faithful: A 365-day devotional.* Thomas Nelson. https://books.google.com/books?id=OYIoDwAAQBAJ&dq=%E2%80%9C.

5   Sproul, R.C. (2011). *Now that's a good question!* Tyndale Momentum (Original work published 1996).

look. Satan shows up, and the first words out of his mouth are, "Did God really say?" This has been his attack for thousands of years. Satan isn't very creative, but he is relentless. He doesn't have to be creative. He doesn't need more weapons, arguments, or cunning approaches. The first shot worked as intended in the garden and it still works today. Why do we doubt God's word?

So, could we have done better? No. The only two humans to ever walk this earth who had a "chance" would be the first two God created. They were picked by God to represent us. His choice. I will gladly take God's choice over mine any day on anything. Adam and Eve had everything going for them. If they failed, we would have failed.

Another way to look at this is to consider what God did to restore the relationship between Himself and His children. As a result of the crucifixion, it is now possible for us to step boldly to the throne. "Let us then approach God's throne of grace with confidence, so that we may receive mercy and find grace to help us in our time of need" (Heb. 4:16). Love requires a choice, free will. We may complain about being related to Adam and Eve, but God more than made up for the problem. As we are related to the first Adam, we can now be related to the second Adam. 1 Corinthians 15:21-22 reads, "For since death came through a man, the resurrection of the dead comes also through a man. For as in Adam all die, so in Christ all will be made alive."

Only Emotional
Weaklings Need Religion

"We may ignore, but we can nowhere evade the presence of God. The world is crowded with Him. He walks everywhere incognito."
—C.S. Lewis[6]

Another typical criticism to our faith is from the group of proud souls that believe they are strong enough to face life and whatever happens on the other side by themselves. They don't "need" religion, the ultimate narcotic. Christianity, or perhaps they would say *all religions*, is man's attempt to give us hope, some confidence, that we are not here by ourselves. Clearly, we are more than pinballs—magically appearing by chance out of thin air like cosmic accidents. We use our faith as a crutch to limp along a nasty road filled with potholes and ultimately leading to a dead end. Perhaps God will save us from the earthquakes and tornadoes.

So, did God create man, or did man create God? From a Christian perspective, what we know about God comes from the Bible. But the Bible is not entirely "good news." If man made up the narrative between the front and back covers, certainly we would have written a far better—better for us—adventure. One where God was confined to being a loving father, a Santa Claus on steroids. Certainly we would limit His omnipresence (do you really want God everywhere?), His omniscience (we would prefer to hide many things from Dad), and His omnipotence (well, if we need Him to steer a hurricane to the east that would be great, but this seems a bit of a dangerous idea one way or the other).

If man did create the Bible, again, the foundation of our faith, the writers most likely would have left out many

6 Lewis, C.S. (2003). *A mind awake: An anthology of C.S. Lewis* (C. Kilby, Ed.). Houghton Mifflin Harcourt.

passages and concepts. Below are some examples:

SIN: Many writers throughout Scripture clearly describe man in a fallen state and that our sin-nature has infected every aspect of our lives (total depravity). One of the best passages that describes this pervasive condition occurs in the Old Testament, where David tells us in Psalm 14:1-3 that

> The fool says in his heart,
> 'There is no God.'
> They are corrupt, their deeds are vile;
> there is no one who does good.
>
> The LORD looks down from heaven
> on all mankind
> to see if there are any who understand,
> any who seek God.
> All have turned away, all have become corrupt;
> there is no one who does good,
> not even one.

TRADITION (history as recorded outside of Scripture) claims that each of the disciples was martyred, with the exception of John, who most likely died of old age. They each experienced a horrible death. Since no one dies for a lie, their martyrdom proved they wrote what they believed and witnessed.

HELL is described as a very real place where those who end up there are tormented forever. As Jesus says in Matthew 13:42, "They will throw them into the blazing furnace, where there will be weeping and gnashing of teeth." And as Revelation 21:8 reads, "But the cowardly, the unbelieving, the vile, the murderers, the sexually immoral, those who practice magic arts, the idolaters and all liars—they will be consigned to the fiery lake of burning sulfur. This is the second death." Jesus, in Matthew 7:21-23, certainly gets our attention by warning us that even those who "claim" to be Christians may spend eternity in hell. In my estimation, these three verses are the most frightening in the entire Bible. We can assume that, if man is making up a religion, the hell concept, especially as threatened by the founder— the high-priest—most likely would be the first to go.

And GOD'S HOLINESS? And His justice? What? No explanation is needed but to recall the times in the Old Testament (prior to the crucifixion of Christ) that God's holiness required an immediate death penalty as punishment. One example occurs in 2 Samuel 6:3-7 as the Israelites were transporting the ark.

> They set the ark of God on a new cart and brought it from the house of Abinadab, which was on the hill. Uzzah and Ahio, sons of Abinadab, were guiding the new cart with the ark of God on it, and Ahio was walking in front of it. David and all Israel were celebrating with all their might before the LORD, with castanets, harps, lyres, timbrels, sistrums and cymbals. When they came to the threshing floor of Nakon, Uzzah reached out and took hold of the ark of God, because the oxen stumbled. The LORD's anger burned against Uzzah because of his irreverent act; therefore God struck him down, and he died there beside the ark of God.

Clearly, if this is a man-created deity, we need a new story writer—a second attempt at a God who is a bit more friendly. God is holy, holy, holy (according to Scripture), and the only way we enter into His presence is through the death of Christ. As Matthew 27: 51 states, "At that moment the curtain of the temple was torn in two from top to bottom." Now, we can step boldly to the throne, like the author of Hebrews 4:15-16 argues, "For we do not have a high priest who is unable to empathize with our weaknesses, but we have one who has been tempted in every way, just as we are—yet he did not sin. Let us then approach God's throne of grace with confidence, so that we may receive mercy and find grace to help us in our time of need."

That is the God-written story. If we created the biblical narrative, we would wield the sword, control the fabricated God like Aladdin and the Genie (getting unlimited wishes), and rejoice in a free ride to heaven no matter who we were or what we did.

The Bible Is Filled with Contradictions

"Two people can accurately represent the same event without covering all the same details. That's the kind of thing we find in Scripture. Difference does not mean contradiction."
—R.C. Sproul[7]

We hear, periodically, of those who have attempted to read the Bible but have stumbled over what they believe to be contradictions. Elsewhere, in defending the Bible, I have made various comments regarding Scripture being God-breathed, and, if authored by God, it cannot hold mistakes. The contradictions which I will very briefly address here are something different. Simply put, a contradiction is a statement that presents two thoughts, conversations, descriptions, or alleged actions that cannot be true at the same moment. From an etymological perspective, this is called against-speak. To get to the conclusion quickly, what we loosely (and incorrectly) call a contradiction in the Bible is simply a variation, different perspective, or added information.

Many will insist that the writers of the four Gospels contradict each other, but if their intent and target audience are remembered, this accusation quickly dies an early death. Recall, Matthew—written by Matthew—is focused on the Jewish population and, therefore, emphasized the Old Testament Scriptures and prophecies. Mark, most likely written by Mark with Peter pushing the pen, was constructed to alert the Romans that a king had touched down. Luke, the doctor with his scientific and medical training and experience, was detail oriented, systematic, dry, and offered a letter that included

---

7   Sproul, R.C. (2016, March 1). Difference or contradiction? *Tabletalk: One Another.* https://tabletalkmagazine.com/article/2016/03/difference-or-contradiction/

more information about Jesus—the man and His life events—than the others. And, lastly, John clearly emphasized the deity of Christ and, therefore, took on a somewhat different focus or perspective.

Consider that if each of these books, the four Gospels in particular, said the exact same thing, everyone would throw a fit accusing the authors of simply getting together in a back room and conspiring to tell the same story. I recall a joke I used more than once over my years in management. I cannot believe I am admitting to this even in jest. "It doesn't matter if we lie. We just all have to tell the same lie!" Now, dear reader, before you bring this book to Half-Priced Books for a rebate, please be assured that was a joke.

The four canonical Gospels created by the four writers were God-breathed. The authors were carried along by the Holy Spirit. But God did co-labor with them and did not extinguish their styles, their personalities, experience, and natural abilities. Does that make sense?

Honestly, in my mind I see only one "apparent" contradiction worth discussing. And it is a big one. Huge. It has been delightful (and somewhat traumatic) to talk with Christians who, after years of studying the Bible, will announce significant, almost debilitating concern, over what they see (incorrectly) as the gaping hole—the chasm between the nature of the Old Testament God and the New Testament God. The pain and discouragement I feel in just writing that sentence is significant. This is how the story unfolds.

> The Old Testament God is so quick to punish, and when He does, it is so severe. At times, He demanded that the Israelite armies wipe out everything and everybody, not only the enemy soldiers but young men, women, children, animals, everything. It's like He is out of control. But then Jesus is so loving, so peaceful and patient with us. And then He dies on our behalf. What more could He have done?

Well, terrific question, "What more could He have done?" but what is the problem with the discourse above? I guess it is something like a car accident. You can witness normal traffic for a year, but you will always remember the day you witnessed an accident. A more careful read of the Old Testament clearly describes God as being incredibly loving and patient. Certainly, if we wielded that power, we would have put down the rebellion sooner, quicker, and deeper than our loving and patient Father.

When we hear Jesus speak, we have a tendency, for numerous reasons, to remember His most agreeable words and the ones that hold us up and put down the obvious troublemakers, such as the Pharisees. Jesus said, "Woe to you" eight times in the book of Matthew. This was a warning (a divine judgement) that unless they turned, repented, they were doomed to hell. Not a casual wake-up call or suggestion to behave. Nothing He said could have had a deeper bite. Here is one example. Matthew 23:13 states, "Woe to you, teachers of the law and Pharisees, you hypocrites! You shut the door of the kingdom of heaven in people's faces. You yourselves do not enter, nor will you let those enter who are trying to." Also, consider these words aimed at the same target in Matthew 23:33: "You snakes! You brood of vipers! How will you escape being condemned to hell?" Yikes! And John 8:44 says, "You belong to your father, the devil, and you want to carry out your father's desires. He was a murderer from the beginning, not holding to the truth, for there is no truth in him. When he lies, he speaks his native language, for he is a liar and the father of lies." Ouch! But, in my opinion, by far the most difficult—nay, painful—words spoken by Jesus, are recorded in Matthew chapter 7. Please, read that chapter.

My plans are to write a separate piece on the times when Jesus and the apostles really stepped forward with scathing and, honestly, frightening words. No attempt at duplication here. My intent is only to discourage casual talk, stumbling over the concept that God in the Old Testament was so much different than Christ. Not true. So, necessarily then, not a contradiction.

What Happens to the Person Who Has Never Heard of Christ?

"Surely, the question for us to answer. . . is not, May the heathen be saved without the gospel, but Will we be saved if we do not give the gospel to the heathen?"
—Charles Spurgeon[8]

Another struggle people often have with our faith, unbelievers and believers alike, is the question regarding the eternal destiny of those who were never "fortunate" enough to hear the good news—the Jesus Story. How could they possibly be held accountable for not accepting Christ if they had never heard of Christ? As is true with many of the objections, asking these questions—if generated by a compassionate heart, a well-meaning stance, or perspective—is not only warranted but invited. To grasp biblical truth on any subject will most likely lead us to a better understanding of our Lord and a greater appreciation and love for Him. There are clear answers to these questions. As with each topic brought forward in this writing, the recommendation will always be that the reader chase down the many excellent books available. For now, I will simply tell you how I deal with this problem.

What is often embedded in the topic we are contemplating—and I believe accentuates the difficulty in resolution—is a conscious or, perhaps, even subconscious, dividing line drawn between the spiritual haves and have-nots. Let us not assume

8   Robins, H.E. (1891). *The Harmony of Ethics with Theology: An Essay in Revision.* University of Chicago.

that if you live, let us say, in the Bible Belt of the American South, that you are somehow automatically privileged and should easily get caught up in the parade or wave honoring our Lord and Savior. Somehow, this indicates the way to Christ has been made easy. The assumption may be that it is almost impossible to resist becoming a Christian. Compare this with the Muslim, Hindu, or Communist regions of the world, for example, where the light, the Christian Church, is struggling in these oppressive cultures. We can easily conclude that a truly searching individual has reduced options since the Christian Church may not even be able to engage in public practice in any real sense, making it necessary to exist underground. Compare this to Dallas and Atlanta, for instance, where there are numerous Christian radio stations, many safe evangelical churches with open doors, and multiple Christian bookstores with stacks of Bibles. Is a person born here at an advantage? Can we assume the way is easier? At least for now, Christians in the U.S. are not under the stress that our brothers and sisters are experiencing in many parts of the world—at least for now. But the substantial and, perhaps, overriding influence of man-centered religion and the prideful pursuit of the intellectual, along with economic prosperity, have always created a significant barrier or obstacle to the faith, which obviously is not the case in the poorer and more "restricted" societies. Also, let's consider that the overall health of the Church, where there is opposition and persecution, is always better than where there is not. So, the light shines brighter, the salt is saltier, the magnet draws stronger, in areas that are oftentimes seen as being at a spiritual disadvantage. All this to say, the stress points experienced by one who is searching are simply different, but just as dangerous from an eternal perspective.

Bottom line, Jesus came to save us from God's just wrath, and each of us needs the cure, the prescription for the illness that only He can provide. We are all guilty. Guilty of what? Sin, of course, but what sin? Rejecting God, the Father. People who haven't heard of Christ are still guilty of rejecting God.

The wrath of God is being revealed from heaven against all the godlessness and wickedness of people, who suppress the truth by their wickedness, since what may be known about God is plain to them, because God has made it plain to them. For since the creation of the world God's invisible qualities—his eternal power and divine nature—have been clearly seen, being understood from what has been made, so that people are without excuse.
(Rom. 1:18-20)

Let's look at this from another perspective. If a person who dies and has never heard of Christ is truly innocent and, therefore, automatically makes it to the right side of eternity, then we *must* shut down all missions. If we do not, we would be responsible for putting these souls in eternal danger by giving them the option to reject the Savior. The last thing we would want to do is remove or disturb their "innocence."

Again, the truth is we are all guilty and each one of us must declare Christ as our personal Lord and Savior as in Acts 4:12, which states that "Salvation is found in no one else, for there is no other name under heaven given to mankind by which we must be saved," and Romans 10:9-10, "If you declare with your mouth, 'Jesus is Lord,' and believe in your heart that God raised him from the dead, you will be saved. For it is with your heart that you believe and are justified, and it is with your mouth that you profess your faith and are saved."

Why Hell?

"If sinners will be damned, at least let them leap to hell over our bodies; and if they will perish, let them perish with our arms about their knees, imploring them to stay, and not madly to destroy themselves. If hell must be filled, at least let it be filled in the teeth of our exertions, and let not one go there unwarned and unprayed for."
—Charles Spurgeon[9]

Perhaps the most frequent challenge to the Christian faith centers on the pain and suffering of people, especially those who are the weakest, undeserving, or most vulnerable. Our inability to reconcile a loving God who either cannot keep us from harm or one who simply cares not to, creates a distance—a buffer zone, gap, or ravine—not easily crossed. Closely following that dilemma while sharing the emotional intensity is the inability to understand how this loving God could send someone to hell, a place of eternal torment. Hell, apparently to most, would seem too harsh a punishment, regardless of the magnitude of the crime. If God is one who leans toward forgiveness, as is commonly conveyed by the Church, then, certainly, not forgiving someone forever—regardless of the transgression—makes little sense.

There exists a multitude of avenues that can be taken to answer the challenge. Likely the most tried, with varying success, is the explanation of God's character—who He is: that He is not just holy, but deemed holy, holy, holy in Scripture. When our sin is discovered, the rebellion confirmed, the disease of total depravity recognized, even a casual attempt at commingling who we are and God's holiness results in an enormous tension that cannot be brought into balance or conformity. I have briefly

9   Spurgeon, C. (1860). The wailing of risca. The Spurgeon Center for Biblical Preaching at Midwestern Seminary. https://www.spurgeon.org/resource-library/sermons/the-wailing-of-risca/#flipbook/

written about this in *Letters from Tony*, so my preference here is to take a very different approach—one I honestly believe may be easier to contemplate or digest by those who are inclined to conclude no one is bad enough to qualify for eternal punishment as the Bible clearly indicates is possible.

First, let's be sure we understand that hell was created for Satan and the fallen angels, the demons—not people. This is key to understanding what follows. Recall Jesus' words as recorded in Matthew 25:41. "Then he will say to those on his left, 'Depart from me, you who are cursed, into the eternal fire prepared for the devil and his angels.'" The end of the story is accentuated in the Apostle John's book in Revelation 20:10. "And the devil, who deceived them, was thrown into the lake of burning sulfur, where the beast and the false prophet had been thrown. They will be tormented day and night for ever and ever." My guess is that most people seriously considering spiritual matters would not argue strongly against an eternal destiny too severe for Satan and the demons that joined him in their rebellion and attempted coup. See Isaiah 14:12-15 and Ezekiel 28:12-19. God certainly has the authority to pass judgment on such a vile undertaking.

Now, the question becomes what is in the heart of man. One of the most clearly stated conditions of the heart was captured by David in Psalm 14:1-3. "The fool says in his heart, 'There is no God.' They are corrupt, their deeds are vile; there is no one who does good. The LORD looks down from heaven on all mankind to see if there are any who understand, any who seek God. All have turned away, all have become corrupt; there is no one who does good, not even one." God, through David, tells us plainly of the universal condition where all have fallen short. Consider also Jeremiah 17:9. "The heart is deceitful above all things and beyond cure. Who can understand it?" And Romans 1:21 states, "For although they knew God, they neither glorified him as God nor gave thanks to him, but their thinking became futile and their foolish hearts were darkened."

It is clear from the biblical record that in our natural (fallen) state we share many traits with the dark side. And we know, even from experience, that it is possible to spend our entire lives following Satan and the demons' lead. If so, why would we not continue our earthly trajectory into eternity? We are simply exercising our God-given free will to our detriment. Why would we expect the Lord to override our decision to push Him away? Whether we are living life or at the end of life changes nothing. Time falls away to eternity. The measurements of time in the physical world, such as the rising and setting sun, appointments, the watch on your wrist, hunger and tiredness, are no longer present. Without them, time still exists but is no longer divided. Without the physical world and the initial existence of this life, forever is the only option. It makes no sense to be in eternity and declare a term for our destiny. Also consider that sin (rebellion) or, as R.C. Sproul (2008) called it, "cosmic treason,"[10] against an infinite God clearly demands an infinite punishment, a life sentence.

If left in this condition, we would all walk into a frightening world next. God is omnipresent. He is in hell, but we are separated from His goodness, His provision, and we will experience His eternal judgment and wrath. But consider now the rescue. The option to avoid this outcome and spend eternity in the fullness of all our God has to offer has been provided. Let us not be guilty of saying that God sends people to hell. We go there willingly. But the good news—the gospel message—is that God made it possible to avoid that destiny by making a new path. God provided a way to escape hell and get to heaven. If you choose to ignore that path, don't blame God. As Romans 3:22-24 reads, "This righteousness is given through faith in Jesus Christ to all who believe. There is no difference between Jew and Gentile, for all have sinned and fall short of the glory of God, and all are justified freely by his grace through the redemption that came by Christ Jesus."

---

10   Sproul, R.C. (2008, May 1). *Cosmic Treason. Ligonier Ministries: Articles.* https://www.ligonier.org/learn/articles/cosmic-treason/

There is Only One God, Not Three

"The doctrine of the Trinity teaches that God is one in essence and three in person, so He is one in one sense and three in another sense, and that does not violate the categories of rational thought or the law of non-contradiction."
—R.C. Sproul[11]

"Ironically, while modern-day Islam rejects the Gospel accounts as corrupt, the Koran itself commands Muslims to read the Injeel—that is, the Gospel accounts of the life of Jesus."
—Michael Youssef[12]

I recently spent some time in Boston preparing to fly to the Azores. On one of our jaunts around town, we were picked up by a driver, a Muslim, who was originally from Syria. The usual pleasant "Lite and Polite" conversation occurred during our short trip. After unloading the rest of the family at our hotel, I walked up to the driver's window. He had already heard something of my recent trip to Israel, and my desire to help the Syrian refugee situation, so our conversation certainly didn't catch him by surprise. He was a hardworking, young, family man with a couple kids and was now quite at home in New England. We talked about our faith, the Bible, and how the recent tensions in the Middle East were just not acceptable. He expressed, very clearly, a frustration with the polarization between various religious groups. Why couldn't the Jews, Muslims, and Christians

11   Sproul, R.C. (2000). *The holiness of God.* Tyndale Momentum. ALSO SEE: Sproul, R.C. (2010). *Classic teachings on the nature of God.* Hendrickson Publishers AND Sproul, R.C. (2011). *What is the Trinity?* Reformation Trust Publishing.

12   Youssef, M. (2015). *Jesus, Jihad and Peace: What does Bible Prophecy Say about World Events Today?* Worthy Books.

get along? What was the big deal anyway? Were we not all after the same thing?

At that point I asked him if he had read the Christian Bible. *Christian* was my way of separating the New Testament from the Old Testament, which I could have mislabeled the *Jewish* Bible, but I was simply trying to communicate. He replied that he had read various parts and was actually pleasantly (my word) surprised. So, laid up on the rim, I asked him what he thought about Jesus. Our conversation went south, not deep south, but south. Asking for some clarification, I sensed that if Jesus was indeed just a good man, a teacher, preacher, maybe at most a second-tier prophet, he could accept that, but the concept that he could be God was clearly offensive.

It is interesting to me that the *Qur'an* tells us that Jesus is certainly a prophet and, according to traditional Islam, never died. Apparently, Allah made another man look like Jesus so his enemies would crucify someone else (Qur'an 4:155-158, 6:85-91, Goodword Books edition). Jesus actually ascended into heaven (physical or spiritual) and will be a key participant in an eschatological climax sometime in the future. What my new friend from Syria was unable to consider was that Allah himself would enter human history in the form of a man. Also, because there is only one God, the concept of the Trinity—God existing in three Persons—was impossible to grasp.

Now, this brings us to the frequent criticism, the reason for this short essay: How can God, if He is one, be three? Again, another subject not easily dealt with in a few paragraphs, but this is the best I can do.

First, the Old Testament confirms there is One God. Deuteronomy 6:4 states, "Hear, O Israel: The LORD our God, the LORD is one." Let us assume the "majestic plural" is invoked in the various verses where God is presented as "us" rather than the passage being a direct reference to the Trinity. This has been debated by conservative theologians for many years, and, therefore, the likelihood of us resolving the issue now is exceedingly small. Let us choose to emphasize the New Testament perspective and leave the Old Testament use of the "royal we" debate for another time—perhaps the other side of the river? And, of course, at that point it won't matter.

In the New Testament, the Father, the Son, and the Holy Spirit are all individually identified as God. First, God the Father is seen in Galatians 1:1. "Paul, an apostle—sent not from men nor by a man, but by Jesus Christ and God the Father, who raised him from the dead." Second, the Son is exemplified in John 5:18. "For this reason they tried all the more to kill him; not only was he breaking the Sabbath, but he was even calling God his own Father, making himself equal with God." And third, the Holy Spirit as Acts 5:3-4 reads, "Then Peter said, 'Ananias, how is it that Satan has so filled your heart that you have lied to the Holy Spirit and have kept for yourself some of the money you received for the land? Didn't it belong to you before it was sold? And after it was sold, wasn't the money at your disposal? What made you think of doing such a thing? You have not lied just to human beings but to God.'"

Perhaps the most powerful verses in the New Testament focusing our attention on this difficult concept is the introduction to John's Gospel. "In the beginning was the Word, and the Word was with God, and the Word was God. He was with God in the beginning. Through him all things were made; without him nothing was made that has been made" (John 1:1-3). This is quite spectacular. Here we have Christ (the Word or Logos) clearly described as God, yet being "with" (distinct from) God.

This is an ideal time to consider, if only briefly, the Trinity as explained by Jonathan Edwards[13]. Edwards was an eighteenth-century New England preacher and theologian who was largely instrumental in the First Great Awakening. Please, understand we are barely skimming the surface of his commentary, which goes like this: God thinks of Himself, as actually you and I can also. When we think of ourselves, the thought is distinct from ourselves, but it is also, to some extent, distorted or incorrect. When God thinks of Himself, the result is a perfect representation of Himself. So, Hebrews 1:3 states, "The Son is the radiance of God's glory and the exact representation of his being." The Son, Jesus Christ, is distinct yet the same. Any two persons make a

---

13   Edwards, J. (2000). *Treatise on Grace: And other posthumously published writings* (P. Helm, Ed.). James Clarke Lutterworth (Original work published 1988).

relationship possible and actually necessary. The joy and love that flows from God the Father to God the Son? The Holy Spirit.

The reader is encouraged to watch "John Piper on the Trinity and the trinitarian nature of humanity," a short, three-minute video available on YouTube. The whole video can be found on Piper's website, www.desiringgod.org.

Many attempts have been made to explain the Trinity by looking at the natural. I have difficulty in accepting the various analogies, but that may simply be another shortcoming on my part. To me, the diverse illustrations create more confusion than clarity. The explanation offered by Edwards may be the best we can do to help us understand something that is essentially beyond our understanding.

You Say Only Jesus Can Get You to Heaven

"The question we should be asking if we are really concerned about God's ways, is not 'Why is there only one way to God?' but 'Why is there any way at all?'"
—R.C. Sproul[14]

"Joseph of Arimathea didn't expect to give his tomb away—and he surely didn't expect to get it back!"
—Janet Denison[15]

"That's another problem with you Christians. Your way is the only way. You *have to* join your church—practice your faith. All religions are essentially the same. To believe otherwise wreaks of narrow-mindedness, arrogance, and narcissism. How can Jesus be the *only* way? What's so special about Him?"

Bingo. The person quoted above made a significant turn or observation after the widespread complaint. And, honestly, this frequent challenge to the faith is totally reasonable and easily understood if you don't see Jesus as He really is—the *biblical* Jesus. If all you hear are the rumors— a great teacher, a charismatic preacher, a respected Rabbi who welcomes everybody and loves everybody—then He "looks" a lot like Gandhi and Mother Teresa, let alone some of the people who started the major world religions or cults.

The short answer to "Why Jesus?" is pretty simple. The contrast between those mentioned or alluded to above and the biblical Jesus must be understood first. Jesus is unique. Consider the following:

14   Sproul, R.C. (n.d.) *Why only one way?* Ligonier Ministries. https://www.ligonier.org/learn/devotionals/why-only-one-way/

15   Dension, J. (2018, December 18). Expect his arrival. *Janet Dension: Teaching authentic faith.* https://www.janetdenison.org/blog/expect-his-arrival/.

BORN OF A VIRGIN. See Isaiah 7:14, "Therefore the Lord himself will give you a sign: The virgin will conceive and give birth to a son, and will call him Immanuel."

PERFORMED MANY MIRACLES, such as calming the Sea of Galilee in Luke 8:24. "The disciples went and woke him, saying, 'Master, Master, we're going to drown!' He got up and rebuked the wind and the raging waters; the storm subsided, and all was calm." He walked on water, as recorded in John 6:18-20. "A strong wind was blowing and the waters grew rough. When they had rowed about three or four miles, they saw Jesus approaching the boat, walking on the water; and they were frightened. But he said to them, 'It is I; don't be afraid.'" Jesus raised the dead. See John 11:41-44.

> So they took away the stone. Then Jesus looked up and said, "Father, I thank you that you have heard me. I knew that you always hear me, but I said this for the benefit of the people standing here, that they may believe that you sent me." When he had said this, Jesus called in a loud voice, "Lazarus, come out!" The dead man came out, his hands and feet wrapped with strips of linen, and a cloth around his face. Jesus said to them, "Take off the grave clothes and let him go."

LIVED A SINLESS LIFE, as stated clearly in Paul's second letter to the church in Corinth, chapter 5 verse 21. "God made him who had no sin to be sin for us, so that in him we might become the righteousness of God."

CLAIMED TO BE GOD, which is apparent throughout Scripture. Let's start with the Old Testament. Perhaps the best known is Isaiah 9:6, "For to us a child is born, to us a son is given, and the government will be on his shoulders. And he will be called Wonderful Counselor, Mighty God, Everlasting Father, Prince of Peace." Many times, as recorded in Scripture, Jesus claimed to be God by accepting worship. See Matthew 14:33. "Then those who were in the boat worshiped him, saying, 'Truly you are the Son of God.'" Luke 24:52 states, "Then they worshiped him and returned to Jerusalem with great joy." John 9:38 records, "Then the man said, 'Lord, I believe,' and he worshiped him." Thomas made a straightforward acknowledgement of who Jesus is and was not rebuked in John 20:27-28. "Then he said to Thomas, 'Put your finger here; see my hands. Reach out your hand and put it into my side. Stop doubting and believe.' Thomas said to him, 'My Lord and my God!'" The people of Jesus' day understood exactly what He was claiming. Recall John 10:30-33. "'I and the Father are one.' Again, his Jewish opponents picked up stones to stone him, but Jesus said to them, 'I have shown you many good works from the Father. For which of these do you stone me?' 'We are not stoning you for any good work,' they replied, 'but for blasphemy, because you, a mere man, claim to be God.'"

WAS PUT TO DEATH by the people He came to rescue, as recorded in the book of Isaiah chapter 53 verse 12: "Therefore I will give him a portion among the great, and he will divide the spoils with the strong, because he poured out his life unto death, and was numbered with the transgressors. For he bore the sin of many, and made intercession for the transgressors." The crucifixion is described in all four Gospels. Consider simply Matthew 27:50. "And when Jesus had cried out again in a loud voice, he gave up his spirit."

CAME BACK FROM THE DEAD. Luke 24 tells the story of the resurrected Christ perhaps best. It is suggested that the reader review this chapter. Also, Paul, in his masterful job debating the Corinthians as to the resurrection of Jesus, reminds the readers that it was still possible to get an eyewitness report from some of those who saw the resurrected Christ—an easy and straightforward way to determine the truth of the resurrection. 1 Corinthians 15:6 states, "After that, he appeared to more than five hundred of the brothers and sisters at the same time, most of whom are still living, though some have fallen asleep."

In other words, He is alive. His tomb is empty. As far as we know, religious leaders such as Muhammad (Islam), Joseph Smith (Mormonism), Charles Russell (Jehovah's Witnesses), Moses (Judaism), and Siddhartha Gautama (Buddhism) never claimed to be God or to be sinless. And, as far as we know, they are all dead.

So, Jesus is the only way for a number of reasons, but perhaps the easiest way to get to that understanding is to recognize His uniqueness in fulfilling over three-hundred prophecies written hundreds of years before His earthly life. As C.S. Lewis argued in *Mere Christianity*, the choices are limited. We can sum up his argument offering only three possibilities: Jesus is Liar, Lunatic, or Lord.[16]

16   Lewis, C.S. (2001). *Mere Christianity.* HarperCollins Publishers (Original work published 1952).

The Church Is Filled with Hypocrites

"Because there is one hypocrite, men set down all the rest the same. I heard one man say that he did not believe there was a true Christian living, because he had found so many hypocrites. I reminded him that there could be no hypocrites if there were no genuine Christians. No one would try to forge bank notes if there were no genuine ones."
—Charles Spurgeon[17]

"Why should I go to church or hang out with those Christians? They think they are such great people, so much better than everyone else. I know for a fact that some of them swear, drink, and act like jerks at happy hour after work. Forget it. The Church is filled with hypocrites."

Yes and no. Yes, there are hypocrites in the Church, but the Church isn't *filled* with hypocrites. There is a slight confusion of terms. The Church is *filled* with sinners—not hypocrites. As long as you don't claim to be someone you are not, you are not a hypocrite. You are a sinner. In fact, in order to "join the club," become a Christian—unlike the local country club—this is a must. That is the only way you understand you need a Savior.

But it is a serious sin. When we fail, we should quickly own up to it and not try to convey that we are someone we are not. The bottom line is how Christians live, speak, and act does affect our witness and people's desire—or lack of desire—to pursue the faith. So, again, it's serious stuff. The best way to gauge the depth of this transgression is to grab a Bible and see what Jesus has to say about it. Even a casual read of Matthew chapter 23 is striking. The word "hypocrite" appears six times, being nearly

---

17 Spurgeon, C.H. (1855). *A Caution of the Presumptuous.* The Spurgeon Center for Biblical Preaching at Midwestern Seminary. https://www.spurgeon.org/re-source-library/sermons/a-caution-to-the-presumptuous/

synonymous with the word "Pharisee," part of the religious ruling class of the day. Check out Matthew 23:25-29.

> Woe to you, teachers of the law and Pharisees, you hypocrites! You clean the outside of the cup and dish, but inside they are full of greed and self-indulgence. Blind Pharisee! First clean the inside of the cup and dish, and then the outside also will be clean. "Woe to you, teachers of the law and Pharisees, you hypocrites! You are like whitewashed tombs, which look beautiful on the outside but on the inside are full of the bones of the dead and everything unclean. In the same way, on the outside you appear to people as righteous but on the inside you are full of hypocrisy and wickedness. Woe to you, teachers of the law and Pharisees, you hypocrites! You build tombs for the prophets and decorate the graves of the righteous.

Yikes. These are some of Jesus's most critical and harsh words in Scripture. Jesus is telling the crowd and reminding us today that the Pharisees appeared to do many good things, but they were only done for show. What we would say today, perhaps, is that they did not "practice what they preached" or "walk the talk." Their hearts were proud, not humble or contrite—the condition that the Lord requires. This is hypocrisy. Our response? Take hypocrisy very seriously.

WARNING LABEL: Don't ever measure Christianity by how Christians act. We're not perfect; Jesus Christ is. We may on occasion fail you. Jesus will never fail you.

ONE MORE THING. When you walk up to the pearly gates and they ask for your name and why they should let you in, don't even think about using the excuse that you didn't accept Christ as your personal Lord and Savior because the guy who lived across the street—who attended church—was a hypocrite. That's not going to work.

Christians Have Done Bad Things in the Past

"All the arts come from God and are to be respected as divine inventions."
—John Calvin[18] (as cited in Harbinson, n.d.)

"Leave the broken, irreversible past in God's hands, and step out into the invincible future with Him."
—Oswald Chambers[19]

This objection is the half-brother of another problem, the accusation that the Church is filled with hypocrites. As is the case in recognizing the sin of hypocrisy, there were certainly times over the years that problems were evident and were allowed to persist. If it were possible to redo the past, many volunteers would make the trip, attempting to right the wrongs. It doesn't work that way, and belaboring the point does not appear to be a good choice. It is my belief that you are better served reading about and contemplating other topics. Some arguments, questions, challenges, and follow-up rebuttals may be worth our time. Certainly, others are not. I am not a historian, so I will make no effort to study the failures or perceived failures of the Church over the last two thousand years.

What I do recall is that the Church was instrumental in many very positive changes that occurred in history. Christianity and the advancement of Western civilization are so well integrated

18   Harbinson, C. (n.d.) *Calvin, the arts, and worship*. ArtWay. https://www.artway.eu/content.php?id=492&lang=en&action=show

19   Chambers, O. (2017). *My Utmost for His Highest:* Classic Edition (3rd ed.). Our Daily Bread Publishing.

that we can assume much of what we have was birthed by a basic understanding of the New Testament—specifically, the teachings of our Lord.

- The development of modern science;
- Nearly all humanitarian efforts;
- The development of orphanages;
- Medical advances and the creation of hospitals.;
- Architecture and cathedrals;
- Public education, literacy, and universities (at least in the beginning—don't get me started);
- Inspiring and bringing art into the world;
- Ending slavery.

So, what must we do today? Apologize for the Christians that came before us? I doubt that will help or make a difference, and, honestly, it shouldn't. There is nothing curative or remedial in articulating misplaced apologies for something someone else has done well in the past. I believe most of us would not challenge the argument that we are not perfect or spotless and have fallen short at times as individuals or participants in various groups, organizations, or even as a country. The focus quite necessarily has to be on today. This is the only time we can affect. The past is gone. Learn from it and decide to do better. The future is God's territory. Trust Him for what lies ahead. If everything we do is done for Him, all involved will win. Colossians 3:17 states, "And whatever you do, whether in word or deed, do it all in the name of the Lord Jesus, giving thanks to God the Father through him."

Nothing New Under the Sun: Part 1

"I defend the Bible the same way I defend a lion. I simply let it out of its cage."
—Charles Spurgeon[20]

The essay that follows is part of a letter recently sent to a couple of friends of a friend. Both Christians, they were attracted to a new approach to our faith, perhaps more accurately, an extension of our faith: one that combines various aspects of Eastern Religion. The new philosophy disregards (overwrites?) the many non-negotiable core beliefs of what we have been calling Conservative Biblical Christianity (CBC). The straightforward, foundational statements of CBC were being reinterpreted based on the assumption that, now, we know better. I have purposefully not identified the new religion, philosophy, ideology, or ism (I truly do not know how to properly refer to the movement—movement!) to make a point. In my failed attempt to be witty, I tried to develop a new name for the proliferation of new religions, but someone beat me to it, as is always the case. After a brief search online, I found a Wikipedia topic, "New Religion Movements." Pretty straightforward and a reasonable way to label the relatively recent outbreak of spiritual derivatives birthed from the world religions and cults. Apparently, we can refer to this grouping simply as NRM. Gotta love those Three Letter Abbreviations! But our focus on the foundational aspects of our faith cannot be compromised with any alternatives. I explain more in the essay.

When I mentioned to various people in the recent past what I planned to do in retirement, I was quizzed more than once

20 Spurgeon, C. (1886). *Christ and His Co-workers*. The Spurgeon Center for Biblical Preaching at Midwestern Seminary. https://www.spurgeon.org/resource-library/sermons/christ-and-his-co-workers/

about my start-up. Start-up what? What was my new "religion" going to be all about? Shocked the first time but not the second, I suggested that there was only one true religion and everything else is essentially a fake—a knockoff, or, perhaps, best described as counterfeit.

This seems an excellent time to insert a short note to my very good friends, members of a Kingdom Hall or the LDS Church. I mean no disrespect by what I have written. I strongly believe that we can agree to disagree when it comes to our faiths and still support each other in our life's journey. No one is being tossed to the curb. In fact, I invite well-meaning, open, and honest conversation anytime and anyplace we may have the opportunity to engage. God loves each one of us. Equally. He has no favorites. Therefore, we should not, either.

The letter: First, please understand that I am a layperson. If I have any thoughts at all that might be worth conveying besides those developed while leading a Bible Study at work, it possibly could be my actual work experience as a petroleum geologist. Pursuing truth for thirty-four years without being able to see the subject under investigation directly, actually, in some ways, is terrific training for pondering complicated issues such as faith— and a lot of fun. They actually *paid* me to go on a treasure hunt. Most people are used to touching, feeling, seeing, hearing the news, and they can accept or deny, believe or reject, based on these strategies. Knowing full well that these tools, our various senses, can fail us at times, we just need to be careful. Often, this approach works fine. But sometimes, encumbered by natural limitations, it does not. We (all of us) embody various defects in our human construction, or, put another way, we are limited by our sin nature. We are blind to various distractions. We don't know what we don't know. We cannot always taste the poison before it is consumed.

Back to business. The targets we drilled for were frequently miles underground, necessitating a careful combination of various remote sensing techniques to help us understand the landscape—actually, the *buried* landscape. Since we were involved in multimillion-dollar decisions nearly every day, the concept of truth was front and center. Even though it had to be inferred from the various clues put together like a puzzle, describing objective reality was the final destination. Granted, especially as time went on, computer-generated 3D visualization aided our natural abilities, but, then, also created a new set of problems sometimes missed until a target was missed. This approach was very different than taking measurements, analyzing, and modeling as an engineer might do prior to construction. During construction, you can always "check" results visually if necessary. We could not until it was too late. Dry hole. Oops.

If we learned anything over the years, we discovered the best solution was often the simplest. We tend to overcomplicate the issues. Why? Not sure. We all do this at times. A likely reason may include some combination of pride and competition. We absolutely hate taking our hands off the steering wheel. But what we don't see, as I suggest above, is best dealt with—if possible—in its simplicity. When we drilled poor wells or dry holes, the "gotcha" elements were actually predicted nearly all the time. The problem was we did not forecast the chance of occurrence properly. But we "saw it coming." To put the concept in spiritual terms, consider Romans 1:20. "For since the creation of the world God's invisible qualities—his eternal power and divine nature—have been clearly seen, being understood from what has been made, so that people are without excuse." As Christians, we can see with more clarity "what's coming."

A long introduction simply to say there are various ways to determine what is ultimately true, but the best way, regardless of the subject, is to measure, analyze, and model with the tools given to us in *Scripture*. There have been volumes written on the authoritative (canonical) nature from cover to cover of our current translations, inerrancy of the original manuscripts, and fulfilled prophecies. Basically, *Sola Scriptura*. It seems to me that the subject today may be an attempt to look *beyond*, to add to, or, at least, to integrate various perspectives. Maybe this can be viewed as remote sensing (let's call it heart knowledge and experience) or some extension of man-generated philosophy. Is this the case?

The Bible is incredibly straightforward. See 2 Corinthians 4:1-4 at the end of this essay (at the end of "Nothing New Under the

Sun Part 3"). It can lead us ahead with great results when we yield our hearts fully—leveraged significantly by the Holy Spirit and the process of illumination. I would be very interested in hearing your perspective as to why Scripture may or may not be complete or contain the answers necessary to live a life pleasing to God and understand the world around us.

And one more point before we get "started." Recall the Lord's words as spoken by Solomon, "What has been will be again, what has been done will be done again; there is nothing new under the sun" (Eccl. 1:9).

Nothing New Under the Sun: Part 2

"It is their failure to bow before divine law, the will of God regarding faith in Jesus, that renders them practitioners of lawlessness—and guilty."
—Thomas L. Constable[21]

O ver the decades, I have tried to understand the truth claims of the various religions birthed here in the States in the nineteenth century, specifically, the Jehovah's Witnesses and the LDS Church. Each, in one form or the other, takes the position that Jesus, His disciples and, by logical extension, the New Testament Church somehow dropped the ball. Various heresies in the early part of the first millennium infected the faith with a terminal disease that derailed God's intentions. I find that quite difficult to swallow. If we believe any part of the Scriptures, we know that the Cross of Christ is central to everything. That is not hyperbole. Jesus could not have "dropped the ball." I have said in other places that *we practice an intensely boring faith* in that what we have believed for nearly 2,000 years hasn't changed—nor will it ever! It is this perspective we should address first rather than the actual elements of any new thought or knowledge. Agreed?

From the PBS website (emphasis added):

Affected by the great religious excitement taking place around his home in Manchester, New York, in 1820, fourteen-year-old Joseph was determined to know which of the many religions he should join. He encountered a passage in the Bible instructing any who lacked wisdom to "ask of God" (James 1:5). Early one morning in the spring of 1820, Joseph went to a secluded woods to ask God which church

21 Constable, T. (2020). *Notes on Matthew: 2020 edition.* Plano Bible Chapel. https://planobiblechapel.org/tcon/notes/pdf/matthew.pdf.

he should join. *According to his account, while praying Joseph was visited by two "personages" who identified themselves as God the Father and Jesus Christ. He was told not to join any of the churches.*[22]

We can easily understand how this could not be true from a CBC perspective.

Ironically, from the Jehovah's Witness (n.d.) website:

While Russell took the lead in the Bible education work at that time and was the first editor of *The Watchtower,* he was not the founder of a new religion. The goal of Russell and the other Bible Students, as the group was then known, was to promote the teachings of Jesus Christ and to follow the practices of the first-century Christian congregation. Since Jesus is the Founder of Christianity, we view him as the founder of our organization.[23]

The Jesus of the JWs is not the biblical Jesus. The JWs are a "new" religion, not the true Church or an improved version of the New Testament Church. They are not a "Reformation Phase II."

Here's one more brief comment on JWs and the LDS Church. One evening I was having dinner with two young Mormon guys. We had a great conversation for literally five and a half hours. Being approximately midnight, we tossed their bikes into the back of my son's pickup truck, and I drove them home. The only time they appeared to be thrown off by my questions occurred when I said to them, "Okay. I get it. But why shouldn't I just become a Jehovah's Witness?" No answer from the two guys that, believe me, had an answer for *everything.* Why? It doesn't matter. The ultimate choice is not between JWs and LDS. It is between Conservative Biblical Christianity and everybody else.

From a different perspective, please consider the likelihood

22   PBS (n.d.). *Joseph Smith: 1805-1844.* American Prophet Bibliography. Retrieved from https://www.pbs.org/americanprophet/joseph-smith.html

23   Jehovah's Witnesses (n.d.). *Who was the founder of Jehovah's witnesses?* Retrieved from https://www.jw.org/en/jehovahs-witnesses/faq/founder

that Adam and Eve were the two most brilliant people to walk this earth and we are the, well, the most challenged. Let us be careful. If we accept Darwinism or the various offshoots made necessary by the inherent difficulties in his thesis, we can easily infer that our knuckle-dragging ancestors were not capable of understanding much of anything. Compare this to the enlightened, technologically advanced, twenty-first-century prodigies: Us. Reality may very well dictate the trend is perfectly (180 degrees) contrary to what we assume today. This should be a major hurdle when contemplating any new thought. Do you see why?

Summary to this point:
• • • • • • • • • • • • • • • • • •

- All of us could be wrong at times, except when we believe what God speaks to us.
- *Sola Scriptura.* God speaking to us.
- We're not getting smarter. Good grief. Turn on the TV.

Nothing New Under the Sun: Part 3

"The chief danger that confronts the coming century will be religion without the Holy Ghost, Christianity without Christ, forgiveness without repentance, salvation without regeneration, politics without God, heaven without hell."
—William Booth[24]

Now, the subject—that is, looking at one of the NRMs in the light of CBC.

Jesus is *not* Lord.

Consider, "You know the message God sent to the people of Israel, announcing the good news of peace through Jesus Christ, who is Lord of all" (Acts 10:36).

Jesus is *not* the Savior of the world.

Consider, "But our citizenship is in heaven. And we eagerly await a Savior from there, the Lord Jesus Christ" (Phil. 3:20).

Jesus was a special Jew. Jesus's death on the Cross was not to pay the price for our sin. It was just a love gesture. What more could anyone do to exhibit love? Pure unity. Sin and salvation are not relevant concepts. They have no meaning and need not be dealt with.

A good starting point here is the C.S. Lewis (2001) argument, often times referred to as the "Lunatic, Liar, or Lord" trilemma. Jesus wasn't simply a nice person or great Rabbi. He didn't give us that option. Also, consider, "'He himself bore our sins' in his body on the cross, so that we might die to sins and live for

24 Funk, I.K., and Gregory, D.S. (Eds.). (1902). *The Homiletic Review. Andover Theological Seminary,* 44(790), 382. https://books.google.com/books?id=GtUnAAAAYAAJ&pg=PA382&lpg=PA382&dq=william+-booth+chief+dangers&source=bl&ots=Oaxy7r_7Iz&sig=9VN9g_JMjtr-JdbQUJ77dLyMOx8M&hl=en&sa=X&ved=0CEoQ6AEwBzgKahUKEwjM-rarUoeLGAhUNEZIKHUXYC3A#v=onepage&q=william%20booth%20chief%20dangers&f=false.

righteousness; 'by his wounds you have been healed'" (1 Peter 2:24). Also see, "Salvation is found in no one else, for there is no other name under heaven given to mankind by which we must be saved" (Acts 4:12).

The Bible is *not* the Word of God. It is *not* inerrant. Scripture is subservient to experience.

Many people prefer to interpret Scripture like "their" Jesus did. Christ apparently ordered from the buffet, picking and choosing what looked good at the moment. They challenge the Holy Spirit by wondering if Jesus (not knowing Greek) would agree with His words written in the New Testament, which was written in Greek. See 2 Timothy 3:16, which states: "All Scripture is God-breathed and is useful for teaching, rebuking, correcting and training in righteousness, so that the servant of God may be thoroughly equipped for every good work."

The Holy Spirit is somewhat analogous to the Force in *Star Wars*. "It" flows in us.

As the Apostle Obi-Wan Kenobi says, "It's an energy field created by all living things. It surrounds us and penetrates us; it binds the galaxy together," also, "You can't win, Darth. If you strike me down, I shall become more powerful than you can possibly imagine."[25] While we are here, consider, "Only a Sith deals in absolutes."[26] It's a great line which obviously is stated as an absolute, but let's skip over that and consider Jesus' words: "Whoever is not with me is against me, and whoever does not gather with me scatters" (Matt. 12:30). Sounds absolute and seriously dualistic. Speaking of which. . .

Dualistic thinking (good and evil in opposition, for instance) is a source of many bad things, so this is not to be considered. Likewise, being saved or not saved is dualistic and, therefore, detrimental. No sin, no savior. CBC warns us clearly that a form of dualism exists. We simply need to be "on the right side," so Isaiah 5:20 warns, "Woe to those who call evil good and good evil, who put darkness for light and light for darkness, who put

---

25   Lucas, G. (Director). (1977). *Star Wars: Episode IV - A new hope* [Film]. Lucasfilm Ltd.

26   Lucas, G. (Director). (2005). *Star Wars: Episode III - Revenge of the Sith* [Film]. Lucasfilm Ltd.

bitter for sweet and sweet for bitter." When God says "Woe," we need to take Him very seriously.

May I add at this point: This sounds like parents telling their kids everybody is a winner. Every kid gets a trophy. Ultimately, everybody wins. Apparently, a major portion of the NRMs are essentially derivatives of universalism—all roads lead to God.

To discover our "True Self" or the "Real You" is to experience heaven. In biblical terms, there is a literal heaven and a literal hell. Matthew 5:12 says, "Rejoice and be glad, because great is your reward in heaven, for in the same way they persecuted the prophets who were before you." Also, 2 Corintihans 5:1 speaks in similar terms: "For we know that if the earthly tent we live in is destroyed, we have a building from God, an eternal house in heaven, not built by human hands." And Matthew 23:33, there are these words: "You snakes! You brood of vipers! How will you escape being condemned to hell?'"

I see (not being an expert here, I see somewhat darkly) shades of New Age, Hinduism, and Chinese religion and tradition. To confuse us further, in Taoism and Confucianism, the concept of yin and yang is paramount, which appears to be duality on steroids. Regardless, everything is connected. There is an energy that flows throughout, whether it be in us or generated within a tourmaline crystal. (Sidebar: Any geologist would rather have a specimen of tourmaline than quartz, the most common mineral on the planet. I couldn't resist saying that!) Again, think *Star Wars*. But even in *Star Wars* there was a chosen one (ironically, born of a virgin) destined to bring balance to the Force.

As stated earlier, we cannot add in any way to our faith. Sometime between A.D. 81 to 96, the Apostle John wrote the following,

> I warn everyone who hears the words of the prophecy of this scroll: If anyone adds anything to them, God will add to that person the plagues described in this scroll. And if anyone takes words away from this scroll of prophecy, God will take away from that person any share in the tree of life and in the Holy City, which are described in this scroll. He who testifies to these things says, "Yes, I am coming soon."

Amen. Come, Lord Jesus. The grace of the Lord Jesus be with God's people. Amen.
(Rev. 22:18-21)

Postscript

· · · · · · · · · · ·

Therefore, since through God's mercy we have this ministry, we do not lose heart. Rather, we have renounced secret and shameful ways; we do not use deception, nor do we distort the word of God. On the contrary, by setting forth the truth plainly we commend ourselves to everyone's conscience in the sight of God. And even if our gospel is veiled, it is veiled to those who are perishing. The god of this age has blinded the minds of unbelievers, so that they cannot see the light of the gospel that displays the glory of Christ, who is the image of God.
(2 Cor. 4:1-4)

Friends and Tony Ping Pong: Part 1

"Vainly do they run about with the pretext that they have demanded councils for the faith's sake; for divine Scripture is sufficient above all things."
—Saint Athanasius of Alexandria[27]

Before we get started, please, know: I respect these guys, my friends. When it comes to raw brain power, they leave me in the dust. They are asking great questions and making excellent, well-thought-out comments. And they are believers. My challenges are well-meant from my heart. That being said, you may very well think I came on a bit too strong. Maybe. Maybe not. When it comes to choosing sources of ultimate truth, there are not many options. Well, there is only one. And here comes some Carvalho sarcasm. Something I usually throttle back on but decided (hopefully prayerfully) that this may be a time to engage. You may think my patience was wearing thin in parts of my responses. That wasn't the case. The Yankee in me occasionally escapes. The downside to reading any book is you cannot see the body language—the smile on the author's face. I am smiling.

This is my full conversation with my friends, verbatim besides small, grammatical edits. Don't worry; they gave me permission to publish our discussion in this book:

FRIENDS: I am just saying I enjoy logical arguments that also use MORE than just Scripture.
TONY: So, logical arguments, man-generated logical arguments, outweigh God's voice? His thoughts? Please, define the word "enjoy." I enjoy eating ice cream. I don't think that is what you mean. I am thinking you mean "am

27   Donaldson, J., Roberts, A., Schaff, P., & Wace, H. (Eds.). (1892). *Nicene and Post-Nicene Fathers, Second Series.* Christian Literature Publishing.

intrigued by" or "interested in." You have got to decide, Epistemology 101, where truth ultimately resides—in man or in God? Do you really think we can outthink—debate with—God? What happened to Job? He tried it. When God shows up, he runs under the table. It was easy to do since, at that point, he was about six inches tall. MORE than Scripture. MORE? Something beyond. Something smarter, more elegant, intellectual? Help me here.

FRIENDS: Tony's entire argument for "Jesus being the only way" is literally just quoting Scripture(s). Literally not one single logical thought about the world, diversity, culture, or even the change of Christianity over the years and the earth during the years the religion has been around.

Brief pause to interject: I have talked with a few people over the decades and have never been accused of using *too much* Scripture. Caught me by surprise. Okay, let's continue:

TONY: This is great. Really. Oh no, *just* quoting Scriptures. My bad. Is Scripture authoritative or not? Yes or no? Sounds like a resounding, "I am not sure." Well, let's stay on point. Again, Epistemology 101, how do we know? The classical arguments are classical because they are definable and logical. Where did we get our ability to be logical? Ultimately from Him, of course. Or from our ancestors, parents, and teachers? Oh dear. Rough sources—each one.

What is Scripture? If you are looking for answers in (from) the world or people or cultures, I would hesitate because that ain't gonna work. Certain questions, such as "What is best on a pizza?" may very well be found there, but the foundational issues—the nature of God; of man; who am I?; ultimate truth; is there a heaven or a hell? Good grief. If you honestly are intrigued or interested in the multitude of viewpoints driven by your desire to understand others and their struggles, great. Go for it. I wish more people would be like that. Ultimately, however, truth resides in God—the Word of God as proven by all the things we have already gone over. *Sola Scriptura.* Why should there be something else beyond God? I think—we think—man can trump (oops) God. I cannot get that out of my noggin. By definition, we cannot. With all respect, we really need to be careful. The first skirmish was ignited by the comment, "Did God really say?" It wasn't much of an argument. We folded in a heartbeat then got tossed out.

FRIENDS: I'm too busy to text today. I appreciate the thoughtful responses. However, I'm dying to get an on-point response from someone on my central question posed now three times which is, (reworded again), If Christianity is the only way to God, then what happens to all the people who never heard about Jesus?

Pause again! This is one of the most typical challenges to the faith that I have addressed in another essay. This, of course, is a legitimate concern, birthed by a compassionate heart searching for an answer to remove what appears to be a difficult challenge to our faith. It is not. Forgive my somewhat flippant response. It is not. Moving on:

TONY: They hear two words after a brief argument at the Pearly Gates, "Elevator down." Because they have rejected God. The Father. Forget Jesus. I can't believe I said that. Guys, this isn't man's world. It is God's world. Next time around, you can make the rules. God is holy, holy, holy, and we're not, not, not. Light and dark together. We're toast. To begin understanding God, we have to first admit He is God, and we are not. You know what kind of God I (we) want, not that it matters? A chubby God—big beard, red suit. One that gives me presents not just on Christmas morning. When you accept Christ, you are indwelt by the Holy Spirit. Anyone want to talk about Jonathan Edwards? When indwelt by the Holy Spirit—from a spiritual viewpoint—you look like Christ. When you show up at the Pearly Gates, you experience a case of mistaken identity. The guys (or ladies) guarding the gate think we are Jesus. They "mistake" us for Jesus.

Final pause: Please, don't take my words literally. I am kidding, of course. Some might rightfully throw a penalty flag and bring this book to Goodwill to at least get a tax write-off. I'm doing the best I can to make a point. We look like Him. And He, the Guy who owns the *joint,* is the only one that gets in because it is His home. More accurately, we are *joint*-heirs—we are adopted into the Family. Okay, one more time:

I *really* want to inject about ten Scriptures at this point.

There are no garbage cans in heaven. You follow me? And we are saved by *grace,* not works. All those wonderful people who have not been reborn, recreated, regenerated, or saved don't get in because they don't look like Christ—the *biblical* Christ. We preach Christ and Him crucified. *We do not get into heaven because God loves us. We get into heaven because our invoice (debt) has been paid. "It is finished" means "Paid in full."* Do you believe that? Yes or no? "Maybe" is fine, perhaps even honest. But, then, we need to move the "maybe" to "yes."

Friends and Tony Ping Pong: Part 2

"If people can be saved and accepted by God the Father apart from the saving work of Jesus Christ on the cross, then why was He crucified?"
—Michael Youssef[28]

TONY: Okay, one more approach. Let's try this. I have heard the story (as you guys may have also) more than once that when persons in central Pangea or Gondwanaland (geologic humor) out in the middle of nowhere get together and say, "Hey, God up there? Hello? Not sure who you are, what you look like, or where you live. We don't know much. What we do know is we have made a lot of mistakes. And we are really sorry. We are kind of confused and lost and really could use some help. Please, do something. Send us someone, so we get to know you." Guess what? You know what happens the following morning? By "chance," a plane full of missionaries with Bibles show up. So, let's go easy on the "innocent" native thing. First of all, they're not. They are anything but "innocent." I honestly believe when lost people remove their pride, arrogance, and narcissistic (will lighten it up) "tendencies," which we are *all* born with, the Good News "magically" appears on the doorstep—if not the next day, someday. Consider this: "The Lord is not slow in keeping his promise, as some understand slowness. Instead, he is patient with you, *not wanting anyone to perish, but everyone to come to repentance*" (2 Peter 3:9, emphasis added).

Our friend, Jim Denison, recently mentioned Sundar Singh, who is a powerful voice for the gospel. We are reminded

28 Youssef, M. (2015). *Jesus, Jihad and Peace: What does Bible prophecy say about world events today?* Worthy Books.

that God is very capable of sidestepping the workers and getting the job done directly. Please, read the entire story on the *High Places Prayer* website. Here is a small part:

> Sundar Singh was born in 1889 into a wealthy Sikh family in Rampur, India. At the age of 14, on the night before a planned suicide, he cried out to God to show himself. Jesus appeared to Sundar in a vision saying, 'I died for you. I am the Savior of the world.' This encounter was so powerful, that Sundar dedicated his life to following Jesus and sharing the Gospel.[29]

And who hasn't heard the terrific news from the Middle East? Striking stories abound suggesting that ISIS is doing their job in spreading the gospel. Their atrocities have apparently jolted many Muslims, essentially forcing them to seriously question their faith and the words recorded in the *Qur'an*. These seekers are contacting the various Christian ministry groups active in the area and describing in great detail similar stories of seeing Christ in a vision or dream with Him directly telling them that He is the Way, the Truth, and the Life (John 14:6). It is commonly reported that more Muslims have come to Christ in the last fourteen years as compared to the last 1,400. That's more than a cute phrase. It is an important truth. Some people believe strongly that the fastest-growing church is now underground in Iran. The Lord graciously allows us to co-labor with Him, but nowhere in Scripture do we see the human element being the ultimate governor to the Holy Spirit's activity.

Sure, I have thought over and over in the past, "*Gee-whiz*, Lord. Does someone go to the wrong side of eternity because of my lazy rear end or because of my deficiency or shortcomings?" *Nope*. They go because they just continue going the way they have been going their whole lives.

29 "Life Invested in Tibet: The Apostle of the Bleeding Feet Sadhu Sundar Singh 1889-1929." (2019). *High Places Prayer.* http://www.highplacesprayer.com/sadhu-sundar-singh.html.

Rebellious little ones who, as we know from Romans chapter 1, get it. They won't get their hands off the steering wheel. They want to take over. Sound familiar? That's what the dark side has been up to from the beginning. And even nice cuddly bears don't get in—whatever nice means. God does not (*cannot*) grade on a curve. Faith, not works. Holiness, not good intentions. A 100 on the Calculus test, not a 97.

And remember, if they are innocent, the last thing we should do is rob them of that innocence by preaching Christ. If they reject the gospel, do they forfeit their innocence? Woe, woe, woe to the missionaries. Call them home as soon as possible! That hasn't been the game plan for about two thousand years. Are you calling for a re-org?

Also, please, do not ever think that we, the pampered American Christians, have it so much better than those poor, lost cultures. The hardest people to "convert" are the "Almost Christians." Guys, please, read (preferably more than once) Jesus' words in Matthew chapter 7 verses. . . wait. I will make it easy. You work and have families. I am retired and have a dog.

> Not everyone who says to me, "Lord, Lord," will enter the kingdom of heaven, but only the one who does the will of my Father who is in heaven. Many will say to me on that day, "Lord, Lord, did we not prophesy *in your name* and *in your name* drive out demons and, *in your name*, perform many miracles?" Then I will tell them plainly, "I never knew you. Away from me, you evildoers."
> (Matt. 7:21-23, emphasis added)!

Look at the Scripture. A good number of counterfeit "Christians" (in the name of Jesus—three times in one verse!) are gonna be toast. Even the "Christians" who prophesied, tossed demons, and did miracles. Imagine what could happen to some portion of our church members and regular attenders. It has been my experience that individuals who are born and raised in a predominantly Muslim culture (for example) may have a better chance of getting to the right side of eternity than many of us here, for instance, in the Bible Belt. Spurgeon so eloquently puts it this way: "Perhaps the only persons who need go thirsty through the street where there is a drinking fountain, are the fine ladies and gentlemen who are in their carriages. They are very thirsty but cannot think of being so vulgar as to get out to drink."[30]

FRIENDS: I'm not saying I don't believe.

TONY: I am a bit confused. Do you believe or not? You cannot (it is not logical to) believe something and deny it at the same time. Do you believe Jesus is the *only* way? Yes or no? I am in the midst of a similar discussion with someone I have known for years. She gets the "Jesus is the only way" thing because that is what He said. Period. But she is having a hard time with it because *well, uh, I kind of, jeez, just don't, ahh, sounds like. . .* have you had enough? She doesn't like it. Why? It's a foreign concept, and perhaps she simply doesn't understand the *uniqueness* of Christ. The basics aren't in the noggin yet. The truth has been flirted with but not resolved or confirmed. And, honestly, *she* may want to make the rules. Maybe she would prefer to toss God off the throne and live *her* way. Not God's way. Not *the* way. God's way is going to be, look, and seem quite different than ours.

You want to be logical outside of the Bible? Okay. Let's do our best to imagine God. That's it. Do the best you can. Forget Scripture. I can't believe I said that. Define God by Googling or just what's in your beanie. Now, define yourself. Any difference? Intellect, approach, capacity, understanding, emotions, yes—spiritual fabric, background, experience, relationships, perspective. Had enough? What we believe

30   Spurgeon, C. (2018). *Charles Spurgeon's Morning and Evening: Wednesday, June 13, 2018.* BibleGateway. https://www.biblegateway.com/devotionals/morning-and-evening/2018/06/13

must be different than God. So, if God believes *X*, there is a great chance—given what I just said—that we will believe *Anti-X*, given our opposite native abilities. That's pretty simple logic and outside of Scripture. You wanna go down the contingent being or aseity tunnel? Probably not. Can't blame you.

FRIENDS: And unless God is cruel and unjust or trivial or there is a second god called chance that also reigns over us, I cannot reconcile the realistic worldview with the strict Christian interpretation.

TONY: Good! Yes! You made it to the finish line, and, of course, you are spot on. You *cannot* and will never be able to (using human logic) reconcile "the realistic worldview with the strict Christian interpretation." Of course not. As Scripture reads, "'For my thoughts are not your thoughts, neither are your ways my ways,' declares the LORD. 'As the heavens are higher than the earth, so are my ways higher than your ways and my thoughts than your thoughts'" (Isa. 55:8-9).

Please, don't forget that God Himself came into human time and space and died the most excruciating death ever over the entire history of the planet, and this was not as bad as carrying the sins of the world, which was not as bad as being forsaken by God the Father. *Breathe*. Don't know about you. But I have a hard time labeling that "cruel, unjust, and trivial." What more can we demand?

FRIENDS: And I don't think I've heard anything even on point of this topic thus far.

TONY: I *respectfully* disagree. You have *heard* it. Just won't *accept* it.

PART TWO:

Putting the Bible First, Sola Scriptura

Scripture, aka
The Users' Manual

"God made us: invented us as a man invents an engine. A car is made to run on petrol, and it would not run properly on anything else. Now God designed the human machine to run on Himself."
—C.S. Lewis[31]

One of the best books ever written by a human not under the authority of the Holy Spirit (i.e., not a part of the canon) is *Mere Christianity* by C.S. Lewis. If you don't have the writing, put this book down, log in to Amazon, and order yourself a copy. If you do and have read it, read it again. The quote above is just a very small sample of Jack's wisdom and perspective referencing our need to understand that we were created by God and He alone knows what makes us run. Put another way, we can only "run" on Him, who He is, what He provides, and what He desires. Anything else spells trouble. Who wants trouble? Apparently, at one time or another, all of us.

As you can tell by now, I simplify everything. I see people (me included, of course) running to the hardware store and buying a lawn mower. We get home and, instead of pouring gasoline in the gas tank, we try orange Powerade. A few attempts at starting the lawn mower fail. If we struggled enough to make the error— no harmful intent assumed—we might brush off the incident. Why did we not look at *The Users' Manual*? Even the "Quick Start" section probably would have told us that gasoline was a better choice.

Take a look at our culture today. You see a lot of people pouring orange Powerade into their lawn mowers. So much of what we fight over, stumble through, agonize about, and debate with

31 Lewis, C.S. (2001). *Mere Christianity.* HarperCollins Publishers (Original work published 1952).

disproportionate intensity could very easily be fixed by even a brief look at *The Users' Manual* for the human being, called the Bible. As Matthew 6:33 reads, "But seek first his kingdom and his righteousness, and all these things will be given to you as well."

God created us and included directions with the purchase on how to maintain the product. Why don't we pay attention to the manufacturer? Well, the answer is simple, of course. We think we know better. There's that pride thing again.

But listen to what God tells us here: "'For my thoughts are not your thoughts, neither are your ways my ways,' declares the LORD. 'As the heavens are higher than the earth, so are my ways higher than your ways and my thoughts than your thoughts'" (Isa. 55:8-9).

It is also a great idea to sharpen the lawn mower blade periodically. You can cut through the weeds a lot quicker.

Where Are the Funny Stories in the Bible?

"Can you imagine Jesus going to dinner parties and never laughing? Can you picture him changing water into wine to keep a wedding party rolling and never cracking a smile? Can you fathom a master story teller who never used humor?"

—Don Sweeting[32]

I have sometimes wondered, if God is the author of humor, why there are not more stories and verses in Scripture that make us laugh. Perhaps a partial reason is the humor is embedded deeply in the ancient language and culture, and looking for the twist is too difficult to do from where we are now. It may also have something to do with the simple fact that there is no other document ever written that details weighty matters, and with the knowledge of who we are infinitely better than we know ourselves. God may have determined that handing us a good dose of the funny was somewhat analogous to handing off a lit stick of dynamite. We struggle enough at times to understand the essence of what has been revealed to us.

When I read certain passages out of context, they seem pretty entertaining. One example is when Jesus is quoted in Matthew 17:17 it seems that He is frustrated with the guys who are just not getting it. But, if you back up a bit to understand the reason for His words, it becomes obvious that this was not a time to laugh. "'You unbelieving and perverse generation,' Jesus replied, 'how long shall I stay with you? How long shall I put up with you? Bring the boy here to me.'"

Another example is a conversation between God and Moses. Moses tries to convince the Lord He has made a poor choice.

32   Sweeting, D. (2013). *The Humor of Christ.* National Association of Evangelicals. https://www.nae.net/the-humor-of-christ/.

Exodus 4:13 reads, "But Moses said, 'Pardon your servant, Lord. Please send someone else.'" The next verse tells us that God's anger burned against Moses. Again, this is not the time to laugh. But it is the time for us to realize that without God's Spirit in control, we can easily feel defeated and not able. We are right. We are not able, but God is.

I find this verse reasonably entertaining. After Jesus has told the disciples numerous parables, we read in Matthew 13:51, "'Have you understood all these things?' Jesus asked. 'Yes,' they replied." A simple, lonely *yes*? What are the chances the disciples understood *all* these things? Again, funny—but we are in the same mold and, hey, there is hope for us also. In general, the biblical characters are not amazing people. They are average people chosen by God to do amazing things. Again, there is hope for all of us. We just need to be open, available, and willing to be sent.

How about this one? Proverbs 21:9 states, "Better to live on a corner of the roof than share a house with a quarrelsome wife." Possibly not politically correct but funny.

Then there is sarcasm that shows up in a few places. Hey, if God can use it, so can we. A friend of mine who is a pastor reminded me a while back that sarcasm was actually a spiritual gift. Now, that is funny. Job 38:19-21 offers us an example when it reads, "What is the way to the abode of light? And where does darkness reside? Can you take them to their places? Do you know the paths to their dwellings? Surely you know, for you were already born! You have lived so many years!"

But this, by far, is my favorite:

> So Peter and the other disciple started for the tomb. Both were running, but *the other disciple outran Peter and reached the tomb first.* He bent over and looked in at the strips of linen lying there but did not go in. Then Simon Peter came along *behind him* and went straight into the tomb. He saw the strips of linen lying there, as well as the cloth that had been wrapped around Jesus's head. The cloth was still lying in its place, separate from the linen. Finally *the other disciple, who had reached the tomb first,* also went inside. He saw and believed.

(John 20:3-8 emphasis added; Note that three times in six verses how John tells us that he outran Peter. Okay, John, we get it!)

He saw and believed.

Pinball

"Without Him, the cosmos would be chaos, and if He has the power to hold everything together, how could anyone believe that he needs to turn anywhere else to find completion?"
—R.C. Sproul[33]

Simple minds (like mine) need simple metaphors to comprehend much of what we find ourselves pondering. It is my guess that many believers still think of themselves and those around them as pinballs. Pull the plunger back slowly over nine months, then we're shot out into play. The ball seems to ricochet randomly at various speeds, sometimes racking up a great score and sometimes headed straight toward the flippers. A seasoned player can whack the ball back into play, sometimes with a good swat and other times barely hitting it, using both flippers timed perfectly. A great player can nudge the table, keeping the ball in play and avoiding tilting the machine. Playing the game is a lot of fun. Sometimes it is easy. Sometimes hard. Some players are certainly better than others.

But here's the problem. There is nothing in Scripture that suggests we are pinballs jettisoning around in life, being at the right or wrong place at the right or wrong time. Our movements are anything but random. Accidents never happen. We just don't understand, nor can we calculate, the many variables and how they interact at any given moment.

Also, we know we have free will within the larger dance choreographed and empowered by a sovereign Lord. And not one grain of sand is transported by the wind in the "wrong" direction. Consider Proverbs 16:33, "The lot is cast into the lap, but its every decision is from the LORD." Also, Isaiah 48:17, "This is what the LORD says—your Redeemer, the Holy One of Israel:

33 Sproul, R.C. (2011, Jan. 12). The great sustainer. *Tabletalk: The New Testament Epistles.* https://tabletalkmagazine.com/daily-study/2011/01/great-sustainer/.

'I am the LORD your God, who teaches you what is best for you, who directs you in the way you should go.'" How all this happens is beyond us. We cannot begin to understand given our natural human limitations. We have enough problems understanding how to handle a four-way stop or resetting the time on the microwave after a power outage.

If there was a pinball in the Bible, it was our old friend Joseph. He certainly was bounced around throughout his life. But look what the Lord accomplished in his life. And the great news, Romans 8:28, is the ultimate guarantee. No matter what we find ourselves in, Christians, can be certain that the outcome will always be good. And what God calls good is great.

The Scariest
Chapter in the Bible

"No man, in his wits, would choose to go to the gallows, because it is a smooth, pleasant way to it, nor refuse the offer of a palace and a throne, because it is a rough, dirty way to it; yet such absurdities as these are men guilty of, in the concerns of their souls."
— Matthew Henry[34]

"Few will enter the kingdom compared with the many who will perish. Jesus clearly did not believe in the doctrine of universalism that is growing in popularity today, the belief that everyone will eventually end up in heaven (*cf.* John 14:6)."
— Thomas Constable[35]

We rightly view the Bible as a love letter from our Lord. It can also be considered as The Users' Manual. The Manufacturer of the Human Species obviously knows how to keep us running at optimum efficiency. It is also inerrant in the original manuscript. It perfectly records history. It contains the words of Jesus Christ, Immanuel, when He was here 2,000 years ago. The Word is uplifting, encouraging, and promising. But it is also filled with truth—objective reality. It describes the love of God perfectly—His grace, mercy, and justice. Perfectly.

By far, the most unsettling chapter in the Bible, in my opinion, is Matthew 7. The entire chapter, except for the last two verses, records the words of Christ. He is concluding "The Sermon on the Mount." Let's look at the section heading: "The Narrow and

34   Henry, M. (1992). *Matthew Henry's Commentary on the Whole Bible* (Vol. 5). Hendrickson's Publishers (Original work published 1710).

35   Constable, T. (2020). *Notes on Matthew: 2020 Edition.* Plano Bible Chapel. https://planobiblechapel.org/tcon/notes/pdf/matthew.pdf.

Wide Gates." "Enter through the narrow gate. For wide is the gate and broad is the road that leads to destruction, and many enter through it. But small is the gate and narrow the road that leads to life, and only a few find it" (Matthew 7:13-14).

We are being told, in remarkably straightforward language, that many (most) will end up on the wrong side of eternity. Conversely, few will make it to the right side. We recall perhaps Jesus' most direct words of His three-and-a-half-year ministry, "Jesus answered, 'I am the way and the truth and the life. *No one comes to the Father except through me.* If you really know me, you will know my Father as well. From now on, you do know him and have seen him'" (John 14:6-7 emphasis added). All paths do not lead to God—*the* God, the biblical God. Jesus alone is the narrow road. Verse 7 reminds us that He and the Father are one. The only way to God is through God.

But the part of the chapter that could easily keep us awake at night—but shouldn't if we grasp the security that is available to all of us who are truly born again—is Jesus' warning to those who falsely believe they are born again. "Not everyone who says to me, 'Lord, Lord,' will enter the kingdom of heaven, but only the one who does the will of my Father who is in heaven. Many will say to me on that day, 'Lord, Lord, did we not prophesy in your name and in your name drive out demons and in your name perform many miracles?' Then I will tell them plainly, 'I never knew you. Away from me, you evildoers!'" (Matt. 7:21-23). The warning Jesus is clearly stating is simply that many of those who claim to be Christians (in the name of Jesus) won't make it. And, as is often recognized throughout Scripture, when certain passages are repeated, we should take particular notice. If a word or phrase is repeated three times, especially in one verse, write it down! Memorize it! That is as straightforward a warning as any found in Scripture. And while we are here, let us agree, that the "will of the Father" is to *accept the Son.* As it says in John 6:40, "For my Father's will is that everyone who looks to the Son and believes in him shall have eternal life, and I will raise them up at the last day."

And it can be assumed that these individuals are most likely not casual church attenders who read the Bible and pray for five minutes occasionally. They are people who have prophesied, expelled demons, and performed miracles! This also tells us that false believers can do incredible things because of who Christ is—His power, not ours. That is a study in itself with very interesting theological ramifications. Let's return to the warning: people who believe they are Christians may find the gate locked. We can also safely conclude that more than a handful of people will get turned away.

I prefer the ESV here if only for the simple reason that verse 23 is rendered, "And then will I declare to them, 'I never knew you; depart from me, you workers of lawlessness.'" Recall 2 Thessalonians chapter 2, which describes the Man of Lawlessness, the Anti-Christ. I believe our Lord is essentially saying, "Depart from me. I am the Christ. You are of the Anti-Christ spirit." It doesn't get much easier to understand than that.

That's the bad news. In fact, there is nothing worse. But there is good news—in fact, great news! As Christians, our ultimate priority is not to fix the world's problems or simply to love our neighbors. What we can accomplish is a mere trickle. Let us resolve to love and know Christ. The rest will follow in a flood.

Total Recall

"Live every day as if it were your last day. One day, you'll be right."
—Jim Denison[36]

"Aslan," said Lucy, "you're bigger." "That is because you are older, little one," answered he. "Not because you are?" "I am not. But every year you grow, you will find me bigger."
—C.S. Lewis[37]

You want to have fun with someone? I mean, really make them cringe? Get nervous? Remind them that they will have *total recall* in heaven. My guess, only a guess, is that the majority of our Christian brothers and sisters will totally stress, contemplating the possibility that they might have to carry the memory of their failures forever. I have had people remind me—no, *quickly* remind me—of Revelation 21:4, "He will wipe every tear from their eyes. There will be no more death or mourning or crying or pain, for the old order of things has passed away." It may be that most people believe that, when we pass through the Pearly Gates, the metal detector at the door also erases our memories. The verse quoted from Revelation above refers to our then-and-future life in the new Jerusalem, our final resting place. We will, then, live in a "world" where there will be no need to shed a tear—nothing bad will ever happen and we won't sin anymore. Great. But, I believe, we will have a recollection of every single word ever spoken and every thought ever thought. I have a hard time understanding how someone could imagine a world of, yes, robots. With our disks wiped clean we start over?

36   Denison, J. (2019, Apr. 6). *Are we living in the end times?* Denison Forum. Retrieved. https://www.denisonforum.org/resources/are-we-living-in-the-end-times/.

37   Lewis, C.S. (1979). *Prince Caspian: The Return to Narnia.* HarperCollins Publishers (Original work published 1951).

We would all be Adams and Eves. Here we go again—this time with no chance of messing up but also with no chance of loving the Lord in a way that only we can now. We apparently, as the theory goes, conveniently forget our fall and restoration. Or is it just the fall? The whole reason why the Lord created Adam and Eve (they fell, we struggled, He came to rescue us, we struggled some more, and, now, we are glorified) would no longer exist. Our intense, deep, profound love for our Savior wouldn't exist. That's nuts. Of course, we have to know everything, so that we would carry for eternity the depth of Christ's love for His people—the fully restored relationship. Now, the face-to-face relationship would be no big deal if we did not have total recall.

Sidebar comment: On the list is a plan to write up a short, tongue-in-cheek essay on what the garden might have been like if we had never sinned. Spoiler alert: Not good, though most people would probably say, "Hey, great."

Let's take a look at Jesus' words in Luke 7:41-43. "'Two people owed money to a certain moneylender. One owed him five hundred denarii, and the other fifty. Neither of them had the money to pay him back, so he forgave the debts of both. Now which of them will love him more?' Simon replied, 'I suppose the one who had the bigger debt forgiven.' 'You have judged correctly,' Jesus said." And, again, same theme of—for our purposes today—trying to understand what heaven would be like with no sins to be forgiven. Continuing in verses 44-47,

> Then he turned toward the woman and said to Simon, "Do you see this woman? I came into your house. You did not give me any water for my feet, but she wet my feet with her tears and wiped them with her hair. You did not give me a kiss, but this woman, from the time I entered, has not stopped kissing my feet. You did not put oil on my head, but she has poured perfume on my feet. Therefore, I tell you, her many sins have been forgiven—as her great love has shown. But whoever has been forgiven little loves little."

However, let's look at Isaiah 65 verse 17. "See, I will create new heavens and a new earth. The former things will not be remembered, nor will they come to mind." As above in Revelation, you get the idea that the "former things will not be remembered." But recall: Jesus tells us in the Parable of the Rich Man and Lazarus (Luke 16) that the rich man certainly remembers. I have wondered how much Lazarus remembered. Something tells me, everything. Some people have attempted to explain the confusion by recalling the three-step stairwell to heaven: Hades, then heaven, then The New Jerusalem. Maybe there are also depth-of-memory stages along the way. This hurts my head and honestly seems to overcomplicate the issue. For now, the best way perhaps to reconcile the difficulty is to stick with the total-recall theme while also understanding that, once we are in the New Jerusalem, our final resting place, the trivial elements (that don't seem trivial today) will not be remembered. We will be able to recall each, sorry, in excruciating detail, but what difference will it make? Where we are—the overwhelming joy of being in the immediate presence of the Lord—will wipe away every tear. Let's look at this from the opposite perspective. "For our light and momentary troubles are achieving for us an eternal glory that far outweighs them all" (2 Cor. 4:17). Maybe this helps us resolve the question. Paul is saying the hell he faced here—and it didn't get any tougher on many other people—on the other side *wouldn't be worth remembering.*

Perhaps no greater stumbling block could be imagined than to anticipate being in heaven and recognizing that many of our dearest friends and relatives would not be there. Is this an argument for reformatting the disk? No. It is, first, an argument forcing us to get out there and "passionately persuade" all those we know of the truth of Christ. We must share the gospel. Second, we should simply come to grips with the reality that whatever we face in heaven will be entirely understood or made clear by the Lord. We will know Him in such a way that all these speed bumps will be easily resolved. "For now," Paul writes, "we see only a reflection as in a mirror; then we shall see face to face. Now I know in part; then I shall know fully, even as I am fully known" (1 Cor. 13:12).

Back to total recall. Of course, we will have total recall. But,

I humbly suggest, we all don't go out of our way to expand the forgiven items list—total recall or not.

While we are on the subject, ask that someone you just confused whom they would most like to see when they get to heaven. Don't let them say Jesus. We know that. He is and will be the only one that matters. Who else? Really. This can be a light and fun way to start a conversation about the Bible.

I want to talk with King Nebuchadnezzar. Actually, in preparation for that moment, I have been calling him simply King Neb. And honestly, without a spell check, I can't remember how to spell *Nebuchadnazzer*. The interesting thing to me is there may be more conservative Bible students out there that believe he didn't make it to the right side of eternity than those that do. So, this is a challenge. He's there, if at least for these two simple reasons: First, he was in the wilderness eating grass like an ox for seven years. Yes, *seven*. The cake is baked. That's God's signal: he's done. Second, Daniel compared King Neb's dimwit son, King Belshazzar, in a 180-degree or completely opposite viewpoint. "But you, Belshazzar, his son, have not humbled yourself, though you knew all this. Instead, you have set yourself up against the Lord of heaven" (Daniel 5:22-23). Meaning, King Neb (ultimately) humbled himself and did not (ultimately) set himself up *against* the Lord.

But this is all a distraction. My bottom-line reason to talk with him is to simply ask him how anybody could hang out with Daniel for years, see what he saw, and take so long to get it. Good grief. Daniel's the real hero. Hey, wait. Maybe I should talk to Daniel first. . .

Why Are We Compared to Sheep?

"The only safe place for a sheep is by the side of his shepherd, because the devil does not fear sheep; he just fears the Shepherd, that is all."
—A.W. Tozer[38]

A cheetah can run 70 mph in short spurts. My black Lab isn't quite as fast, but I love watching her run. Abbey is very intelligent, funny, and affectionate. Dolphins are sleek, beautiful, and can swim up to 20 mph. Chimpanzees have a terrific memory and use tools. Even pigs, most likely the smartest domestic animals, can be trained more easily than dogs and cats. Sorry, Abbey.

So, what's up with sheep? Sheep are really dumb. Impossible to train. There are numerous reports of sheep literally going off a cliff and plunging to their deaths by the hundreds (sometimes over a thousand)—following their leader. Not a very smart one. This apparently is pretty hard on the first few hundred guys, a lot softer on the last few hundred. This is the definition of "herd mentality." They follow the leader, regardless of the results. Sounds familiar.

Sheep have no natural defense. They cannot fight, run, or bark. Their only hope is that, when the predator gets to them, it's too full from eating their buddies. That's their primary "defense" mechanism. They need a shepherd. Without a shepherd's constant care, they are filthy animals. They are not even capable of licking or caring for their own wounds.

38   Tozer, A.W. (2007). *The Mystery of the Holy Spirit* (James L. Snyder, Ed.). Bridge-Logos. https://books.google.com/books?id=KfIK28QeA-sC&pg=PA158&lpg=PA158&dq=&source=bl&ots=fn7KtnWzW0&sig=ACfU3U0Jel4Z-rY_VihRvHIG_gJ2UwIUQJA&hl=en&sa=X&ved=2ahUKEwjyw5zZ86juAhVIOK-wKHRmfCwo4ChDoATAFegQIBhAC#v=onepage&q&f=false.

They must be good at something. Actually, they are great at aimlessly wandering around, then getting lost—even when they have all they need right in front of them. Oh yeah: They are apparently great at drowning.

The Lord compares us to sheep for very simple and straightforward reasons. We share common characteristics. That's the bad news. The good news: we are incredibly valuable and loved sheep. Let's look at Luke 15:3-7.

> Then Jesus told them this parable: "Suppose one of you has a hundred sheep and loses one of them. Doesn't he leave the ninety-nine in the open country and go after the lost sheep until he finds it? And when he finds it, he joyfully puts it on his shoulders and goes home. Then he calls his friends and neighbors together and says, 'Rejoice with me; I have found my lost sheep.' I tell you that in the same way there will be more rejoicing in heaven over one sinner who repents than over ninety-nine righteous persons who do not need to repent."

I am thinking that, if ninety-nine sheep were paying attention and doing what was right and one took off, we would, given our human shortcomings, shrug our collective shoulders and murmur under our breath, "Oh well." What the Good Shephard does is say, "You guys stay here. Don't go anywhere. I am going to find your idiot brother." Even if this means putting His life in danger, He tracks down the one that wandered away. As Jesus says in John 10:11, "I am the good shepherd. The good shepherd lays down his life for the sheep."

Also worth our consideration is that shepherding was one of the lowest positions the wealthy landowners needed to fill. Commonly, the youngest son in a family, or simply someone of no regard or stature, was called to this menial job. Jesus as our shepherd takes on again the role of a humble and lowly servant. This is somewhat similar to the lowest house servant, tasked with the job of taking off the sandals and washing the feet of other family members and guests. We read in John chapter 13 verse 5, "After that, he poured water into a basin and began to wash his disciples' feet, drying them with the towel that was wrapped around him."

We are helpless. We need our Good Shepherd. We need Christ. Every moment of each day, let's listen for His voice. John 10:27 ays, "My sheep listen to my voice; I know them, and they follow me." And, then, we can say with King David, "The LORD is my shepherd, I lack nothing" (Ps. 23:1).

The Cross of Christ

"We can never fathom the agony in Gethsemane, but at least we need not misunderstand it."
—Oswald Chambers[39]

"It costs God nothing, so far as we know, to create nice things; but to convert rebellious wills cost Him crucifixion."
—C.S. Lewis[40]

We all know the story. But it is too easy for us to focus on what we can come closest to touching, closest to experiencing. Don't get me wrong. We can never experience anything—not a sliver, not a miniscule part, a grain—of the Cross. We relate to the physical agony because each of us at some time has experienced some level of pain and the dreadful imagery of the Cross is something we can see in literature, art, and movies. The pain and agony experienced by Christ overwhelm anything any person had ever experienced or would ever experience. Jesus chose when to die. Any human so severely beaten would have succumbed, fainted into unconsciousness, and then quietly passed away.

Isaiah, in chapters 52 and 53, describes the suffering servant with more precision than any other passage in the Old Testament: "Just as there were many who were appalled at him— his appearance was so disfigured beyond that of any human being and his form marred beyond human likeness" (Isa. 52:14).

As horrific as the physical experience was, it may be that the agony of carrying the sins of all those that would confess Jesus as Lord was many times greater. Imagine Christ—perfect, sinless, pure, without blemish—the lamb who was love incarnate, gentle, and kind. This Holy One received the burden of our impurity—

39   Chambers, O. (2017). *My Utmost for His Highest:* Classic edition (3rd ed.). Our Daily Bread Publishing.

40   Lewis, C.S. (2001). *Mere Christianity.* HarperCollins Publishers (Original work published 1952).

the rebellion. The One who never lied, never lusted in His heart for anyone or anything, never experienced jealousy or hatred, became the sin-bearer, the scapegoat. As Paul explains in 2 Corinthians 5:21, "God made him who had no sin to be sin for us, so that in him we might become the righteousness of God."

We know from various passages throughout Scripture that God cannot look at or tolerate sin. Habakkuk 1:13 reads, "Your eyes are too pure to look on evil; you cannot tolerate wrongdoing." And consider 1 Peter 3:12. "For the eyes of the Lord are on the righteous and his ears are attentive to their prayer, but the face of the Lord is against those who do evil." In addition to Isaiah 52 and 53, the most detailed messianic prophecy that describes the crucifixion is Psalm 22, in particular verses 14 through 18. The first verse of this psalm, initially spoken by David then later by our Lord fulfilling the prophecy, is the passionate cry, "My God, my God, why have you forsaken me? Why are you so far from saving me, so far from my cries of anguish?" He is experiencing hell, the full wrath and punishment of God. Jesus is alone, abandoned, forsaken. This was the ultimate horror of the Cross, not the physical agony. This, and only this, makes it possible for us to step boldly to the throne. This, dear reader, is how much God loves you.

Should We Fear God?

"You're my friend and You are my brother even though You are a King."
—Martin J. Nystrom[41]

"Surrounded by Your glory. What will my heart feel? Will I dance for You, Jesus? Or in awe of you be still. Will I stand in Your presence? Or to my knees will I fall. Will I sing hallelujah? Will I be able to speak at all? I can only imagine. I can only Imagine."
—Bart Marshall Millard[42]

Christians know there are no contradictions in the Bible. There are, however, certain statements, verses, or concepts that may "appear" contradictory. We have all heard the debate regarding our fear of God. There are many verses that clearly state that we should fear God. Enormous wisdom and protection are available to us when we live in that posture. But are we called to fear God or just carry around a healthy dose of reverence? My guess is the current opinion is the broadly accepted attitude that the word "fear" (as translated in our modern Bibles) really means "elevated respect."

We recall Abraham's victory when told to sacrifice Isaac. "'Do not lay a hand on the boy,' he said. 'Do not do anything to him. Now I know that you fear God, because you have not withheld from me your son, your only son.'" (Gen. 22:12). Regarding Joseph, in dealing with and ultimately forgiving his brothers, Genesis 42:18 states, "On the third day, Joseph said to them, 'Do this and you will live, for I fear God.'" The Lord's words to the adversary when He pays Job the ultimate compliment (Job 1:8): "Then the LORD said to Satan, 'Have you considered my

41 Nystrom, M. (1984). *As The Deer* [Song]. Maranatha! Music.

42 Millard, B. (1999). *I Can Only Imagine* [Song]. On The Worship Project. Fair Trade Services.

servant Job? There is no one on earth like him; he is blameless and upright, a man who fears God and shuns evil.'"

But let us not forget Isaiah's reaction to seeing the Lord in the temple. "And they were calling to one another: 'Holy, holy, holy is the LORD Almighty; the whole earth is full of his glory.' At the sound of their voices the doorposts and thresholds shook and the temple was filled with smoke. 'Woe to me!' I cried. 'I am ruined! For I am a man of unclean lips, and I live among a people of unclean lips, and my eyes have seen the King, the LORD Almighty'" (Isa. 6:3-5).

Clearly, someone who fears God is to be commended. By extension: this sounds like the position we should strive for each day. However, throughout the New Testament we are told that He is our brother, our friend. He died for us. Took our penalty. Saved us from God's righteous wrath. "Greater love has no one than this," Jesus says, "to lay down one's life for one's friends. You are my friends if you do what I command. I no longer call you servants, because a servant does not know his master's business. Instead, I have called you friends, for everything that I learned from my Father I have made known to you" (John 15:13-15).

So, maybe we have reconciled the heavy-handed God of the Old Testament and the New Deal, and now we can relax. Take a breath. Who would "fear" a friend that gave His life for us? But then, just when we thought we had it figured out, Jesus speaks with the same "certainty" as God in the Old Testament. Calling us friends, Jesus explains in Luke 12:4-5, "I tell you, my friends, do not be afraid of those who kill the body and after that can do no more. But I will show you whom you should fear: Fear him who, after your body has been killed, has authority to throw you into hell. Yes, I tell you, fear him." Yikes! Don't you want to skip over those verses? Contemplating our future (and permanent) state should certainly invoke an element of fear in us.

Here is another way of looking at it: When Jesus was physically here 2,000 years ago, the reaction of His followers and those of the villages at times would not even remotely suggest "casual amusement." In Luke chapter 8 starting in verse 22, Jesus and the disciples get caught in a violent storm. The disciples are freaking out. After they wake Jesus and He calms the storm, you would think everyone would breathe a sigh of relief and take a nap. This is not what happens. "Where is your faith?" Jesus asked His disciples in Luke 8:25, and the verse continues, "*In fear* and amazement they asked one another, 'Who is this? He commands even the winds and the water, and they obey him'" (emphasis added). They are still fearful, but not because of the storm, but because of the majesty, the holiness, and the power of God.

A bit further into the chapter and you already know the story. Jesus meets a man who is possessed by a demon, Legion (actually, many demons). The demons, "fearing" Jesus, ask Him if they can go into the pigs. They understand authority. Once in the pigs, the pigs—being most likely the smartest domesticated animals on earth—run off a cliff and drown. "All the people of the region of the Gerasenes asked Jesus to leave them," the following verse reads, "because *they were overcome with fear. So he got into the boat and left*" (Luke 8:37, emphasis added). Again, the presence of our Lord did not always invoke a group hug and laughter. At times when His deity and power were on display, the crowd was gripped by fear, which obviously is not only what happened but should happen.

You know what I fear? We have blown it. We love Jesus so much (greater) and we have some small level of understanding as to how much (greater) He loves us that He has become our best buddy. Friend, Brother. Yes, Absolutely: We can now step boldly to the throne. "Let us then approach God's throne of grace with confidence, so that we may receive mercy and find grace to help us in our time of need" (Heb. 4:16). But that's not the whole story. If we don't fear God, we won't fear sin. Also, let us recall that our Brother not only created the universe; He sustains it. He is omnipotent, omnipresent, omniscient. He defeated Satan. He died the most excruciating death imaginable to bridge the divide that we caused by our failure and our sin. Dear reader, this is serious stuff. Let's reset the scale and put Jesus where He belongs. Above, beyond, holy—and to be feared.

Perfectly Timed Geological Episodes

"As the fear of God is the beginning of wisdom, so the denial of God is the height of foolishness."
—R.C. Sproul[43]

One of my favorite responses to out of the ordinary events is to simply ask, "What are the chances of that happening?" Some events are clearly choreographed by the Lord as opposed to natural occurrences. Please do not misunderstand me, especially this early on! Everything that occurs is empowered by the Lord. He is Sustainer (Heb. 1:3). He makes all things possible. What I am trying to partition are those actions that are common from those that require our special attention. When a bird lands on the beach then flies away a few minutes later, I do not seek in earnest and passionate prayer a reason for the sighting and its theological or, at least, spiritual implications. Other things are meant to grab us. They announce the Lord's special communication or provision.

Some continue to deny or oppose our understanding of what we term miracles as recorded in Scripture. For now, let's consider only a few of the ones that involve a spectacular redirect or control of the physical world. Some suggest that these "miracles" can now be explained due to our better understanding (chuckle) of geological processes. Let's look at a few.

Moses Parting the Red Sea: Exodus 14
· ·

You know the story. Moses and the Israelites, with the Egyptians in pursuit, come to the Red Sea. A number of researchers have "explained away" the miracle by modeling and witnessing strong

43   Sproul, R.C. (2011). *Essential truths of the Christian Faith.* Tyndale House Publishers (Original work published in 1992).

winds in the area in excess of sixty miles an hour that literally can move enough water to result in aerial exposure of the sea or lakebed. We could go on and on about this, but the point I would simply like to make here is: What are the chances of that happening? Great timing. Let's look at Exodus 14:21-22. "Then Moses stretched out his hand over the sea, and all that night the LORD drove the sea back with a strong east wind and turned it into dry land. The waters were divided, and the Israelites went through the sea on dry ground, with a wall of water on their right and on their left." It goes without being said that a "wall" of water on their right *and* their left is pretty difficult to explain no matter how much wind there may be. Obviously.

The Death of Jesus: Mark 15

As verse 33 reads, "At noon, darkness came over the whole land until three in the afternoon."

This one actually is tougher to explain away than most people believe. Passover occurs at a time of the month that would make a full solar eclipse impossible. And there is no way the eclipse, unless God made it so, would last three hours. So, we are left with all sorts of Class B explanations, like volcanic eruptions, sandstorms, or a really cloudy day—all of a sudden! Same bottom line. What are the chances of the noonday sun being blotted out right during the final hours of our Lord's life on earth? This was simply the Lord's way of communicating to all of us the darkness of our sin. This event was the focal point of all history. It was the turning point. All time points either forward or backward to this moment.

The Walls of Jericho: Joshua 6

Consider verse 20: "When the trumpets sounded, the army shouted, and at the sound of the trumpet, when the men gave a loud shout, the wall collapsed; so, everyone charged straight in, and they took the city."

This is a favorite of mine, of course, being a geologist. To prepare for my trip to Israel in the summer of 2018, I spent some time reading about the local and regional geology of Israel. Specifically, my interest was to learn what I could about the Jordan Valley Rift system, a significant (on a global scale) geologic feature. The Dead Sea, Jordan River, and Sea of Galilee are surface features created by this major plate boundary. History indicates, as we would expect from current mapping and interpretation, that there have been numerous large earthquakes in this area. Josephus[44] writes about an earthquake that occurred in 31 BC that killed over thirty-thousand people. In AD 749, the Galilee Earthquake had an estimated magnitude of well over 7. The last large event in Israel took place in 1927. Significant earthquakes have occurred throughout history on the average of eighty to one hundred years. Jericho, by my crude estimate (Google Maps), is only five miles west from the surface expression of the system.

There is little doubt that when the "trumpets sounded" that the Lord's creation cooperated, and, within a short distance of Jericho, a major tectonic event occurred bringing down the wall. So, explained: They just got lucky, of course.

---

44   Josephus, F. (1737). *The Wars of the Jews* (W. Whiston). Sacred-texts.com (Original work published 78)

Lessons Learned from the Thief on the Cross

"Oh, Adam's sons, how cleverly you defend yourselves against all that might do you good!"
—C.S. Lewis[45]

"When the time comes to die, make sure that all you have to do is to die."
—Jim Elliot[46]

At times, we are all guilty of being skeptical. In fact, being skeptical as opposed to naïve or gullible is probably a positive trait. When we hear of deathbed conversions, I don't know about you, but I have been guilty of raising an eyebrow. A tap on the shoulder by the Spirit usually puts me in a better frame of mind, but, of course, it takes Him to do it, not me.

Most people in our culture are probably universalists, thinking that all well-intentioned roads lead to God. But there very well could be the opposite spiritual error. Some may believe that we must carry a vast knowledge to impress God enough to break through the Pearly Gates. This would require some length of time to possess. This could be a relative of the most abundant error: that we are saved by works—works here being a deep or profound spiritual understanding "that will certainly get God's attention." Another error.

How long must we be developing our faith before getting in? Apparently, not very long. It's not a time element. It is a simple understanding of who Christ is and what He is offering us. We

45   Lewis, C.S. (1979). *The Magician's Nephew.* HarperCollins Publishers (Original work published 1955).

46   Elliot, J. (2002). *The Journals of Jim Elliot.* Baker Publishing Group (Original work published 1978).

accept the gift made possible only by His death on the Cross. Boom. Done.

The thief on the cross first "heaped insults" on our Lord as recorded in Matthew 27:44. Sometime later, perhaps after watching and listening to Jesus—wrestling with his own agony knowing he would soon die—he realized his error. He understood enough of who Jesus was to be guaranteed a spot in heaven.

> One of the criminals who hung there hurled insults at him: "Aren't you the Messiah? Save yourself and us!" But the other criminal rebuked him. "Don't you fear God," he said, "since you are under the same sentence? We are punished justly, for we are getting what our deeds deserve. But this man has done nothing wrong." Then he said, "Jesus, remember me when you come into your kingdom." Jesus answered him, "Truly I tell you, today you will be with me in paradise." (Luke 23:39-43)

The key words appear to be "your kingdom." The thief knew they would all die and enter into eternity. Jesus was King this side and *the other side of the Cross*. We do not know how much of Jesus' teaching the thief may have heard prior to this moment. Knowing, believing, and trusting Jesus ("remember me") is all it takes. It doesn't take long to get there. Please, read Matthew 20:1-16, "The Parable of the Workers in the Vineyard."

Can we agree that it is possible to jump into the elevator just before the doors shut? I wouldn't even remotely play this game or take that chance when it comes to our eternal destiny. Being convinced that sometime down the road when you are old and gray you will have the opportunity to pull this off is unwise. Better word? Foolish. "Well, Lord, I guess I better say yes to you now. I may not make it much longer." Today, dear reader, you may not make it much longer. Not a lot of people pass away in their sleep or in a car accident, but some do. Are you prepared to play the odds? Honestly, that's crazy if the answer is yes. And, believe it or not, I have talked to more than one person over the decades that has told me just that. That was *their* decision. If you want some excitement, I recommend buying a motorcycle. Or jumping out of a plane, preferably with a parachute. I suppose without one would be more exciting. Even that would make more sense than gambling with your eternal life.

The good news: even though you may be doing a lot of horrible things, making a lot of really bad mistakes, the Lord is ready to forgive you. "Remember me" is all it takes. What are you waiting for? Do it. Now.

Ask the Author

"First of all you must understand this, that no prophecy of Scripture is a matter of one's own interpretation, because no prophecy ever came by the impulse of man, but men moved by the Holy Spirit spoke from God."
—John Piper[47]

Imagine you are sitting in a pub in Oxford in the late 1940s. The sign over the door said something like "Eagle and Child," but you are not sure. You ducked into the pub too quickly to notice. Glad to be indoors, for it had been drizzling for hours, you order and then search through your bag for something to read as a distraction. Through the pipe smoke you see a back room with some men enjoying a pint (or more) and realize these are the Inklings which you have heard so much about. In fact, a portion of the collection of papers now on your table were written by Jack Lewis, which will later be published as *Mere Christianity*, but, for now, your scattered notes are based on some of the BBC presentations aired in the early 1940s. Various pages leave you uncertain, wondering what the author had in mind. Not presented in dry theological terms, the logic was intriguing and certainly thought-provoking. You read, then reread, a paragraph. Questions overwhelm the reader, so you pause, then, gently put the papers away. You finish your supper, a hearty helping of bangers and mash, and another pint, and then give one last attempt to understand the writings.

Wait. You mutter to yourself, suggesting you are a fool. You have no idea how it was possible to struggle this long, when there was little doubt that the author, the creator of the work, was sitting with his friends a mere ten meters away from your table. Of course, you must plead confusion and limited ability,

---

47 Piper, J. (1982). *Men moved by the Holy Spirit spoke from God.* Desiring God. https://www.desiringgod.org/messages/men-moved-by-the-holy-spirit-spoke-from-god.

repenting of trying to do it your way for the last few hours. As you ask him for even a brief moment of his time, Mr. Lewis would be able to explain what was on his heart when he first spoke, then later published, the work. You gather your papers and make your way across the pub, interrupting the gentlemen now just relaxing, teasing each other relentlessly, and enjoying their friendship. Apologizing with unnecessary passion, you make a simple request; "Please, help me understand what you meant when you said. . . ."

Demons and Centurions

"Who is this man that comes my way? The dark ones shriek. They scream his name. Is this the one they say will set the captives free? Jesus, rescue me."
— Casting Crowns[48]

Many of those that surrounded Jesus, even the twelve, occasionally cycled in and out of a state of confusion. They heard Jesus teach, witnessed Him doing miracles, and yet remained unsure. They remained unconvinced that He was the Son of God—the long-awaited Messiah of the Old Testament. Of course, we smile at this and wonder why, but also realize that we have the entire New Testament writings and 2,000 years of hindsight. But something in us still wonders, why?

Anyway, what intrigues me much more than the twelve stumbling over themselves, as I am sure each one of us would have done, are the two groups of "people" that pretty well had Jesus pegged in some ways right away.

THE DEMONS: Satan's fallen angels took one look at Christ and *immediately* knew who He was. First, they knew the facts, and, second, knew they were true. Obviously, they didn't take the third and final step. They didn't embrace, respond to in love, were drawn to, or desire to pursue the Truth. They do the complete opposite. But the certainty that they displayed is indicative of the enemy we face. These guys understand exactly who He is. How could we doubt? What is there to debate?

Let's look at one example in Scripture. Let's start with the struggling disciples. Matthew 8:23-25 states, "Then he got into the boat and his disciples followed him. Suddenly a furious storm came up on the lake, so that the waves swept over the boat. But Jesus was sleeping. The disciples went and woke him,

48   Herms, B., and Hall, M. (2005). *Set Me Free* [Song]. On Lifesong. Warner Chappell Music.

saying, 'Lord, save us! We're going to drown!'" So, get this. A raging storm develops. These guys are fishermen, so, if they are freaking out, this is a bad one. But they are concerned about drowning. With Jesus in the boat?

Sidebar Story: The last project I worked on offshore was keeping an eye on one of the development wells we drilled on High Island Block 384 in the Gulf of Mexico. A "furious storm came up on the lake." I was actually enjoying the ten-to-fifteen-foot wave heights, until the rig hands, who commonly worked in the North Sea and the South China Sea, started showing some signs of anxiety. You don't have to be a genius to figure out that, if these guys are getting nervous after weathering similar (actually much worse) situations, maybe the geologist from the office should start praying instead of taking photos.

Matthew 8:26-27 reads on, "He replied, 'You of little faith, why are you so afraid?' Then he got up and rebuked the winds and the waves, and it was completely calm. The men were amazed and asked, 'What kind of man is this? Even the winds and the waves obey him!'" What kind of man is this? Again, they are confused. Let's continue. "When he arrived at the other side in the region of the Gadarenes, two demon-possessed men coming from the tombs met him. They were so violent that no one could pass that way. 'What do you want with us, Son of God?' they shouted. 'Have you come here to torture us before the appointed time?'" (Matt. 8:28-29). No hesitation. Zero. They knew Jesus was the Son of God and He had authority. Amazing.

As we continue our walk knowing full-well we are involved each day in spiritual warfare, let's remember whom we are fighting. We tend to be confused and hesitant. The enemy is determined, relentless, and single-minded. They are not hesitant or open to negotiations. That's why we need Christ fighting our battles. And we must be fighting with the right weapons. "For though we live in the world, we do not wage war as the world does. The weapons we fight with are not the weapons of the world. On the contrary, they have divine power to demolish strongholds" (2 Cor. 10:3-4).

THE CENTURIONS: Why were those guys consistently way ahead of the Jewish leaders and in some ways even outpacing the disciples? Was it simply the challenging training they incurred and the difficulty in reaching that rank? Or was there more to it? Maybe if we can understand what exactly opened the door for these men, we can extrapolate what we learn today. In other words, who are the modern-day centurions? If we determine the key ingredients in the formula, we may be able to imitate, possibly emulate, the centurions.

One of my favorite chapters in the entire Bible is Matthew chapter 8. A centurion has a servant who is suffering. When this is communicated to Jesus, Jesus simply asks if He should stop by the house with the intent of healing him. The centurion, either from his understanding of Jewish culture and the boundaries between Jews and Gentiles or a deeper understanding of who Jesus is, in humility, responded, "Lord, I do not deserve to have you come under my roof. But just say the word, and my servant will be healed. For I myself am a man under authority, with soldiers under me. I tell this one, 'Go,' and he goes; and that one, 'Come,' and he comes. I say to my servant, 'Do this,' and he does it" (Matt. 8:8-9). Is it really that simple? This centurion seems to know a lot about Christ. He is so certain. Verse 10 tells us, "When Jesus heard this, he was *amazed* and said to those following him, 'Truly I tell you, I have not found anyone in Israel with such great faith'" (emphasis added). I don't know about you, dear reader, but I would absolutely love to *amaze* our Lord. The ESV uses the word "marveled." We recall what we all long to hear someday, "Well done, good and faithful servant" (Matt. 25:21)!

So, what do you think gave the centurions the ability to see Christ more clearly than most? The centurions, in a way like the demons, had significant power. They were not hesitant or open to negotiations and certainly understood Jesus' authority over their power. *Ahhh.* Maybe that is the key ingredient? They understood *authority* in their world and His. Shouldn't we?

Do You Have a Bible Study at Work? Part 1

"Always guard against self-chosen service for God."
— Oswald Chambers[49]

B ack in April of 2002, two ladies from our accounting department came down to see me and kindly suggested I consider leading a Bible Study at Chief Oil & Gas. I was shocked. How could anybody come to the conclusion that I should lead a Bible Study? I had no pertinent degrees and wasn't exactly a biblical scholar. Anyway, I told them I so appreciated their kind thoughts then went on (uninterrupted for about five minutes) to justify my argument that it made little sense for me to accept. Having appreciably more God-given wisdom than I had, they suggested when I got home that evening that I simply pray about it.

Wow. Just pray about it? *Nice*. I agreed.

That night I prayed about it. I spared the Lord the nuisance of listening to the five-minute (now-rehearsed) rebuttal, recalling Exodus 4:13, where Moses asks the Lord to please send someone else, so He got the abridged version. Then I got the Lord's straightforward version that reminded me: (1) The Bible Study was His, not mine. My concentration on what I could not do left Him out of it and made me the center of the effort. *Oops*. (2) The Lord gently reminded me that His children spend very little time in Scripture and, therefore, do not spend time with Him and getting to know Him. If I resolved to make the effort, always being sensitive to the leading and understanding offered freely by His Spirit, I could offer some guidance to the attendees. Also, since I was going to *lead,* not teach, this became more likely.

Do you have a Bible Study at work? If so, great. If not, why

49   Chambers, O. (2017). *My Utmost for His Highest: Classic edition* (3rd ed.). Our Daily Bread Publishing.

not? No employees have attended Dallas Theological Seminary or Dallas Baptist University, have they? (Yes, I lived in Dallas for a couple decades.) There must be some number of believers who would be excited about seeking the Lord at work and praying for your business. I have been told, more than once, that a manager or managers at a workplace may frown upon such an idea. Honestly, it is not worth fearing something that may not even be the case. Come to think of it, don't fear anything. If management frowns on an in-house Bible Study, go to the outhouse. . . I mean, out of house. . . to meet. There is a restaurant or hotel down the street with a room. Deals can always be made, expenses minimized. Christian managers and owners abound. Let me back up for a moment: Also consider that very few people have been caught saying, "Don't pray for me." Convince management that you will be praying for them. They should, without being reminded, figure out (the Lord may help them figure it out) that employees that walk the talk and study the Bible make great employees.

Do You Have a Bible Study at Work? Part 2

"We often become mentally and spiritually barren because we're so busy."
—Franklin Graham[50]

More than once, when we were all scurrying around getting ready for a Bible Study at lunchtime on Wednesdays, someone would come blazing into my office or cut me off on the short journey with a look of apologetic desperation saying, "Tony, I am so sorry. Overwhelmed today. No time for Bible Study." A thoughtful, if not witty, rebuttal would have been appropriate but, at the speed they were moving and the time I need to create a reply, it never seemed to happen.

There is so much wrong with this. And it happened more than I would like to admit. First, the owner of our company, a terrific Christian gentleman who wholly supported the Company Bible Study, would have been disappointed to learn that this was indeed the case. He would have wondered how an employee could justify missing the study to satisfy a deadline imposed by a manager. This is when I was glad to be leading the Bible Study. How could an hour (*one* hour), working for whomever on whatever, be more important than spending an hour with other employees seeking the Lord and praying for our friends, families, management, and each other? Pursuit of the Lord trumps all other endeavors.

Secondly, and more importantly than that, we know we cannot outgive God. There is certainty, we should know, that spending an hour with Him will directly result in an overriding ability to accomplish more. In other words, your efficiency at doing whatever needs to be done is easily compensated for in

50   Graham, F. (2008). *All for Jesus: A Devotional.* HarperCollins Publishers.

proportion to the investment. I have never met anyone who complained about losing something because *he* pursued the Lord first. Recall Matthew 6:33: "But seek first his kingdom and his righteousness, and all these things will be given to you as well." Jesus is talking about what we need to eat, drink, wear, but we can appropriately add: accomplish. In this case, the work we need to get done in any workday will certainly be accomplished, and in a significantly better portion than if we kicked God to the curb and went on our way.

Go to Bible Study. You have one hour per week to honor the Lord at work, no matter what deadline is approaching. If that is *truly* impossible, I suggest you post your résumé on Monster as soon as possible.

Do You Have a Bible Study at Work? Part 3

"The secret of life lies in laughter and humility."
—G.K. Chesterton[51]

"**D**ebbie, would you please close the door." Now why would we do that? Was it because we didn't want our other employees to know we were studying the Bible? *Everyone* at the company was aware of our Bible Study. Perhaps we were discussing a biblical truth that was "controversial" or not politically correct? Recall Romans 1:16: "For I am not ashamed of the gospel, because it is the power of God that brings salvation to everyone who believes: first to the Jew, then to the Gentile." No. We were not ashamed.

We were just having too much fun, and the laughter was certainly capable of disturbing the people who were working through lunch. Many Bible Studies involve a deep (may I call it intellectual) approach to studying Scripture, and there is nothing wrong with that. What we found to be very motivating, and a help not hindrance, is twofold in this regard. There was a bond, a closeness, that was easily created between the brothers and sisters in Christ. That made it easy to laugh and enjoy each other. But also, as we would talk about the various Bible stories, we noticed a frailty in the main players, even those we think of as heroes or spiritually exalted beyond us mere mortals. Many of the characters in Scripture were just that. They were characters! I have written about funny parts of the Bible elsewhere, at least from my perspective, but, if you follow the antics and missteps of a Peter or Moses, for example, you just have to laugh.

What makes this particularly humorous is that we know we are easily capable of similar blunders. Hopefully, and preferably,

51   Chesterton, G. (1919). *Heretics (12th ed.).* John Lane Company (Original work published 1905). https://www.gutenberg.org/files/470/470-h/470-h.htm

we can laugh at ourselves and—in a setting like a Bible Study with the best of friends—laugh at one another.

Imagine the tears of joy and laughter we will shed in heaven.

Do You Have a Bible Study at Work? Part 4

"Beware of any work for God which enables you to evade concentration on Him. A great many Christian workers worship their work."
—Oswald Chambers[52]

Even though I led a Bible Study for many years during my last job, there were a few challenges that remained unsolved. One was homework. And reader, please understand it wasn't that the attendees were asked to argue the validity of predestination, review the five points of Calvinism, discuss the nature of the Trinity, or compare and contrast Arianism and Docetism. Are you kidding? For the first year or so I tried, but then I gave up after much pleading—nay, imploring. The dialogue went something like this:

"Hey guys," (I'm from the New *Yawk* area, so girls are guys too), "next week we will be talking about Matthew chapter 24. When you get a few minutes, *please*, read the chapter over a couple times, and, *possibly*, take a look at a commentary online, *perhaps*, Tom Constable's *Sonic Light*."

Notice, the casual use of *P*s in my Pleading: Please. Possibly. Perhaps. Incidentally, Constable's notes are what I used almost exclusively many times in preparing for the studies.

Next Wednesday's dialogue:

"Hey guys, how many of you had a chance to read over Matthew chapter 24?"

Body language, especially in situations like this, speaks more clearly than any words that could be said. Responses included a variation on the word "what?" Most of the group, guys and girls alike, for some reason decided to investigate what they were

---

52   Chambers, O. (2017). *My Utmost for His Highest: Classic Edition* (3rd ed.). Our Daily Bread Publishing.

wearing that day—on their feet, particularly. What happened? We all do this. Every single one of us. We can easily be Mary during the Bible Study lunch hour and then Martha Martha at home during the week (Luke 10:38-42). How do you solve that problem? Dear reader, I just assigned you homework! Don't fail me!

One of my other challenges (this goes with the territory, of course) was simply attendance. We talked up Bible Study the best we could. *Wait.* Not the best we could, but we "spread the word." Then, someone suggested we do the old bribery thing. "Hey, Tony. How about we just bring in pizza? That should do it. You know. Feed 'em." We normally had four to six attenders. On pizza day we would be searching for conference room chairs, shooting past ten. No pizza. No ten. Back to four to six.

There was another element of the plan. This didn't quite work in my favor. *Oh well.* If only one or two of the "guys" showed up, we would go to lunch. Just us. The problem I was struggling with, especially if we were advancing through a book a chapter at a time, was that we would be leaving the non-attenders behind. So, skip the planned study, go to lunch with the valiant few, and pick up where we left off the following week. Didn't happen often, but it would happen. But I am thinking it backfired occasionally. There may have been some backbench or shadow maneuvering going on. There may have been a plan and some rotation that, occasionally, if going out to lunch sounded like a good idea to two of them, they would "pay off" the third chair, understanding that that person would be next in line for a free lunch. Cannot say for sure, though. . .

Do You Have a Bible Study at Work? Part 5

"Let God have perfect liberty when you speak. Gather your material, and set it alight when you speak."
—Oswald Chambers[53]

There is no doubt that we should be well prepared for each Bible Study: Run through the material, perhaps a few times, and be as organized as our native abilities make possible. Purposefully believing that the Lord will jump in to bail out minimal or poor preparation isn't reflective of a yielded heart desiring to give our all to the One who deserves everything we have to offer. Beyond that, a simple prayer focused on the thought and realization that the attenders need to hear from Him and not from us is clearly appropriate.

It was my ongoing experience, however, that the studies I polished and believed would be the best usually were not. By far, the sessions where we veered off—those going in a direction I could not have predicted—were the best. Why? Pretty simple: Those were especially God-ordained. The self-choreographed chapter-by-chapter deliveries were fine, but the Lord would take over the session occasionally, especially when the Bible Study leader got in a jam. Put yourself in my shoes. Imagine heading toward a chapter in James and ending up being called to referee a discussion on some personal, family matters pertinent to wives and mothers. I am a pretty short guy, but there are times I wish I was even shorter. But the Lord is good. Each time when I found myself clearly in a corner with very little perspective, experience, or witty comments (when all else fails, try humor), my prayers of desperation were answered. And it was startling to watch and hear the discussion that the Lord clearly made

53   Chambers, O. (2017). *My Utmost for His Highest: Classic Edition* (3rd ed.). Our Daily Bread Publishing.

possible. And the Holy Spirit-led insights encouraged each one of us. Every single time.

So, prepare for the studies but stay ready to quickly hand off the steering wheel to the Lord.

Do You Have a Bible Study at Work? Part 6

"I must learn that the purpose of my life belongs to God, not me. God is using me from His great personal perspective, and all He asks of me is that I trust Him."
—Oswald Chambers[54]

One more thing. It usually took me about five hours to prepare for Wednesday Bible studies. The five hours were almost exclusively midnight to 5 a.m. Sunday morning. There were various reasons for doing it that way, but here's the point: Granted in the petroleum industry wells are drilled twenty-four hours around the clock and my metabolism is sky high, pulling an all-nighter has never been a difficult thing to do. But newsflash: I am mortal. I do get tired—sometimes, *really* tired. Being up all night long, watching a well, can be exhausting and a bit stressful.

Each night when I was working up the study and 5 a.m. showed up, I went to sleep because, at that point, you have to make a decision. All-nighter or a few hours of sleep? Another hurdle: you're getting really hungry and whipping up even a quiet bagel with cream cheese would not have been the family's first choice. So, I normally started snoozing at about 5 a.m. or so. The fun part, besides the obvious—spending the time with the Lord—was the simple fact I was *never* tired that day or the following. Obviously, there can be a lag between any effort and the following payment for it. Monday, I was *always* fine.

Is this just because I'm a wound up little Portuguese dude from the New *Yawk* area? More than that. Like I mentioned, staying up out on a well, driving through the night, or being

54 Chambers, O. (2017). *My Utmost for His Highest: Classic Edition* (3rd ed.). Our Daily Bread Publishing.

awake a major part of the night at the house on the phone with the rig drained me at times. Pulling an "almost" all-nighter for Bible Study preps never did. Here's the bottom line: You cannot out give God. What was happening each Sunday early morning for many years was a tradeoff. What He gave back to me for My commitment to study and prepare the lessons for Him? Simply the ability to pull it off. It was His idea anyway.

PART THREE:

Putting Yourself in Scoring Position

Billboards

"The enemy has marked you for annihilation, and his demonic armies are aiming their big guns right at your heart."
—Michael W. Smith[55]

On June 8, 2015, I was driving from Dallas to Rosemary Beach, near Alexandria, Louisiana, going south on I-49. I was listening to Focus on the Family Radio Theatre's production, *Father Gilbert Mysteries*. The actual feature was "Dead Air." Near the end of the presentation, the demon, Legion, leaves a message on Father Gilbert's answering machine. Later, Father Gilbert has a conversation with the demon. This dialogue and the back-and-forth arguments were extremely well acted. The discussion resulted in Father Gilbert reciting the Lord's Prayer and casting out the demon. This exhausted Father Gilbert and brought him to tears. At that point, driving south at 70 mph, I had tears in my eyes also and prayed, "Lord, I understand that the true enemy we face is the dark side, Satan and his fallen angels, the demons." At that very moment, the moment that would normally be an "amen," I looked immediately to my left and saw. . .

55   Smith, M. (2011). *A Simple Blessing: The Extraordinary Power of an Ordinary Prayer.* Zondervan Publishing.

So, what were the chances of that happening? Near zero, of course. I believe the Lord was simply saying "I hear you, and, yes, that is true." This helped. A lot. At that time, it was exactly what I needed to be reminded of. When we wade through difficult moments and trials, it is best to focus on our true enemy and not the people around us. The Lord is good, as Psalm 34:8 reads, "Taste and see that the LORD is good; blessed is the one who takes refuge in him."

Pizzas

"An infinite God can give all of Himself to each of His children. He does not distribute Himself that each may have a part, but to each one He gives all of Himself as fully as if there were no others."
—A.W. Tozer[56]

One day when I was home in Rosemary Beach, I made a quick afternoon trip to the local Publix to do some grocery shopping. That evening, I didn't feel like cooking, so I decided on a pizza. A frozen pizza.

Yum.

I opened the freezer door, and. . . No pizza.

I knew I had bought one at the store, so I was about 80 percent sure it was still in the trunk of my car. *Uh-oh.* It was about 90 degrees that afternoon. Pizza might be baked. Got my car keys, went outside, and popped the trunk, fully expecting to find. . . No pizza.

Well, at that point, I was nearly 100 percent sure I had left the pizza at the check-out counter since, after thinking about it for a while, I remembered not carrying it to the car, it being over-sized and a bit big for a normal plastic bag. Praying with a smile I said, "Well, Lord, I could go back to the store, but I don't think a trip, gas, and time is worth a seven-dollar Margherita Pizza. I guess I can absorb the seven-dollar loss."

A funny moment. As I turned to go back into the house, I looked down on the driveway parking pad and found a ten-dollar bill. So, what were the chances of that happening? Near zero, of course.

I prayed a quick "thank you," and, as always, was amazed that the Lord would provide for me in such a minor or seemingly

---

56   Tozer, A.W. (1979). *Gems from Tozer: Selections from the Writings of A.W. Tozer.* The Moody Bible Institute of Chicago. https://www.google.com/books/edition/Gems_from_Tozer/0lE6AwAAQBAJ?hl=en&gbpv=1&printsec=frontcover.

insignificant way. I am always careful to make sure that these odd things that happen occasionally are from Him, and, also, that I understand and learn all He wants to communicate to me. I was thinking there was more to this episode than a pizza-replacement plan. After this prayer, I received what I call a triple A (Almost An Audible)—a very clear thought that certainly didn't come from me: "Tony, if I am willing to cover your loss of a mere seven dollars, how much more will I cover the loss that you are experiencing now?"

The thought occurred to me to put this very special ten-dollar bill in a shadow box with a plaque identifying the story, date, and source. But the Lord gently reminded me that He is essentially dumping ten-dollar bills on us twenty-four hours per day. We just don't notice. Why, then, was this such a big deal or any different? So, I spent the ten bucks.

Again, Perfect Timing

"Daughter, I have now lived a hundred and nine winters in this world and have never yet met any such thing as Luck. There is something about all this that I do not understand: but if ever we need to know it, you may be sure that we shall."
—C.S. Lewis[57]

Several years ago, while working at Chief Oil & Gas, I thought it would be possible to sneak away from the office periodically and do some extended (adjunct?) teaching at Dallas Baptist University (DBU). If Trevor ever reads this book, it will be the first time he learns of it. I should have known better. They expected me to really work: creating curriculums and outlines and offering hours of dedication and online tutoring. I expected me to casually chat with the students occasionally. One way or the other, I filled out an application, the next step being an interview with Dr. Beverly Giltner, Dean of the College of Natural Sciences and Mathematics. Over a week or so of trading emails and phone calls, we were having difficulty setting something up.

A couple weeks later, I had a meeting with Tammy Williamson, the Director of the Pregnancy Resource Center of Grand Prairie, literally less than ten minutes from DBU. On my way back to the office, I found myself approaching a traffic light after traveling over a bridge near the campus. I prayed the following: "Lord, as You can see, I am headed back to work. When this light turns green, I can go straight and hop on I-30 returning to Dallas, or left, and attempt to track down Dr. Giltner. Let me know what You want me to do." I never say amen anymore for the simple reason: there is no reason to stop communicating with the Lord. Here we go again. At that very moment when I prayed those words (more or less), a few seconds before the light turned

57   Lewis, C.S. (1979). *Prince Caspian: The Return to Narnia*. HarperCollins Publishers (Original work published 1951).

green, my cell phone rang.

"Tony. Jamie here at DBU. Hey, I just got a call from the Dean's office. She has some time for you today. Can you swing by?"

My good friend, Professor Jamie Lash, to this day probably doesn't fully understand why I was laughing when I replied, "Sure. In fact, I can be on campus in a couple minutes."

Dear reader, this is the God we worship, the One who sustains all things. This isn't pulling a rabbit out of a hat or mysticism. We shouldn't be overly amazed and surprised at the perfect timing and His constant care. It is simply an example of relationship—asking for His help and experiencing His answers. Right on time. As always.

Of Hurricane Michael

On October 10, 2018, a hurricane made landfall in Mexico Beach, a small coastal town in the Florida panhandle. This town is immediately east of Panama City, a community of about 37,000 people. The destruction inflicted by Michael, the strongest storm to hit the area on record, was significant with sustained winds in excess of 150 mph.

On the other side of the storm, we look back and prayerfully consider the effects. It is easy to say that those living sufficiently east and west of the storm, where damage was minimal or non-existent, were blessed. I have wondered if we are being shortsighted, perhaps confused, when we equate being spared the pain and loss associated with the hurricane to some special treatment of God. A quick read of the Beatitudes reminds us that those who face most difficult times are actually the ones that are blessed (see Matt. 5:2-11). Likewise, the "Love Chapter" reminds us that true love can only occur when pain and disappointment are present (1 Cor. 13:4-7). Stress, difficulties, and pain are seen biblically as opportunities to look up and to simply trust that a sovereign God and Sustainer has choreographed—down to the smallest detail—each outcome, including destruction brought by natural disasters.

As there are no accidents, there are also no random movements by nature. The Deists were not right. Our friends in the insurance industry got it right when they proclaim certain events, such as a hurricane, an act of God. These events are unlikely and appear random from our human perspective and are not preventable. Yet, God sustains the hurricane and so can drive and direct the storm easily. In other words, He can slow the car since it is His foot on the gas pedal. Jesus didn't work overtime with great effort when He calmed the storm on the Sea of Galilee (Matt. 8:23-27). Natural disasters do occur in a natural way. The worst hurricanes occur in the late summer and early fall. Earthquakes occur along major tectonic plate boundaries. We all age. In general, science, as we know it, would not be possible if chaos reigned.

But what are we seeing now? How have things changed? The landscape is altered, but it should only be a reminder of the clearing of the view, a starting point for something new—something elevated—in that our area has a potential to move ahead, to build, and advance in a much more unimpeded way. Honoring the Lord actually is not that difficult, but He has just made it easier. Now is the moment we have, knowingly or not, been asking for. Our prayers can be stagnant and encumbered. The Lord's hand is not. This would have been no one's choice except the Lord's. How we deal with the aftermath, making it into something powerful for Him or not, is a choice we now all face. For each of us a significant opportunity, one we never dreamed of, exists. We are called to co-labor with Christ. Well, He has run well ahead of us and accomplished the heavy lifting. Let's sprint to catch up to where He is so we can share in the victory. May we all hear the words "Well done good and faithful servant" (Matt. 25:21).

How do we do this? Simply trust and embrace Him. Don't look back (Gen. 19:26). Take the time with all those you will see to let them know that you will be participating in the healing and restoration of more than just the physical and emotional needs of the area, but you are determined to work within the context of a spiritual revival. Ultimately, this option yields the greatest (being eternal) rewards. *The true value found in the wake of Michael thus lies in the acceleration of ministry, outreach, and missions.* The Lord has leveled the playing field (literally), turned our attention to Him, and now made it even more possible for us to impact the area and, perhaps, our culture. Let us not think too small—for nothing will be impossible with God (see Luke 1:37). Hurricane Michael has put us on the stage. For whomever is watching, our testimony will be heard like very few times in our past.

There are those who were directly impacted by Michael and those who were spared. The people in its path were blessed beyond those who escaped. This should only remind us that there indeed are only two kinds of people, those taking a right turn at eternity's door and those taking a left.[58]

---

58 First published as the Epilogue in Dr. Jesse Nelson's book *We Survived Hurricane Michael*. Published here with minor changes.

Don't Block
the Blessing

Under the shadow of our steeple.
With all the lost and lonely people.
Searching for the hope that's tucked away in you and me.
Does anybody hear her?
Can anybody see?
—Casting Crowns[59]

Many of us grow up with the idea that it is best to be self-sufficient. We can handle it. "Don't bother yourself. I can do it." *Ouch.* There is that pride thing again.

There's a problem with this. First of all, by waving off the help, you may be blocking the blessing—not only intended for you, but the blessing the Lord intends for the helper. It is always best to avoid the category of lazy (obviously), but that is not what I am referencing. There are certainly times that we should step up and work our tails off, getting ourselves, someone else, or the organization over the hurdles. Sometimes, literally, we have to work day and night. Paul tells us this in his letters, mentioning his efforts not to cause his brothers and sisters an extra hardship—one example being, "Surely you remember, brothers and sisters, our toil and hardship; we worked night and day in order not to be a burden to anyone while we preached the gospel of God to you" (1 Thess. 2:9).

There are many well-meaning Christian friends who desire nothing more than to come alongside of us, especially in a time of need. Whatever that may be. Perhaps the best response (if not our natural inclination) would be to reply thankfully, suggesting specific things that would be helpful. A meal? Two or four more hands moving furniture around the house? Call

59   Hall, M. (2005). Does Anybody Hear Her? [Song]. On *Lifesong*. Warner Chappell Music.

me Mr. Practical. A physical burden relieved. Giving you and your wife a break by watching your kids so you could scoot, occasionally. An emotional burden relieved. You get it. We are all in this together. The health of the Church could be improved if we shared (cheerfully) each other's burdens.

But at the top of the list is praying for someone. Also, we can share the "distractions" of life—the struggles, the disappointments—by encouraging them and simply listening. Perhaps we can offer to be their accountability partner. When moved by the Spirit to come alongside of someone else, we relieve their burdens. The hands and feet of Christ. We do what Jesus did. "Carry each other's burdens," Paul writes, "and in this way, you will fulfill the law of Christ" (Gal. 6:2).

Especially when things get rough, reach out. Let someone help you. Don't wait. Put down the shovel and pick up the phone. Then, when the smoke clears, celebrate together.

I Would Have
Fought to the Death

"Let the wife make the husband glad to come home, and let
him make her sorry to see him leave."
—Martin Luther[60]

"When I have learnt to love God better than my earthly
dearest, I shall love my earthly dearest better than I do now."
—C.S. Lewis[61]

One of my primary reasons in putting together this book was
to take complicated solutions to complicated problems and
reduce them to a common denominator. All of us if not all the
time, many times, are drowning in stuff and getting to closure
or crossing the finish line in record time is a challenge. As I have
mentioned, I led a Bible Study at work. It wasn't a Women's Bible
Study, but, since many of you ladies (sorry guys) tend to be a bit
more "active" in your faith, the attendees were mostly women.
Perhaps one guy. Sometimes two.

One of my canned Bible studies was entitled, "Congratulations,
You Married a Jerk." My simple reason to start at that point was
to toss the gauntlet on the table, suggesting that "we," us guys,
are essentially in many ways the same. Don't make the first error,
automatically thinking you totally goofed, being convinced that
other men in the world somehow would have been a better
choice. *Ha!*

Women have issues. Men have issues. God made us that way. Get
over it. Smile. You are not alone. Easy? Not so easy. You have to trust
Him, cool off, and prayerfully move forward, preferably together.

60   Varvis, S. (2017). Luther's table talk and quotes, and Bach too. *Fresno Pacific
University.* Retrieved (date when source was first found). https://blogs.fresno.edu/
educated-state/2017/06/24/luthers-table-talk-and-quotes-and-bach-too/.

61   Lewis, C.S. (1966). *Letters of C.S. Lewis.* Houghton Mifflin Harcourt.

Here's the simplest way to bulletproof your marriage. Divorce Denier 101. Do these five things, preferably in this order:

1. Never, ever, use the word "divorce" unless you're talking about your neighbor.

2. Tell your spouse he or she will always be number *two*. And mean it.

3. Pray together about everything.

4. Come to a *Full Stop* every so often in the "Being Mom & Dad" department and "Be Wife & Husband." Prescription label: Take the medication at least once per quarter over a three-day weekend.

5. Buy a copy of Gary Chapman's, *The Five Love Languages*, read it and read it again—hopefully with your spouse— and, then, *do it*.

I am certainly not the local marriage counselor, and I have fallen down on the job more than I would like to admit, but I suggest, with all my heart, that the divorce rate would be slashed in half if spouses simply decided to do the five things mentioned above. Why wouldn't you?

Also, recall a marriage agreement is not a contract. It is a covenant, a promise. Contracts emphasize the horizontal (the human element) and release one party if broken by the other. Covenants emphasize the vertical (the spiritual element) and, if broken by one party, the other remains bound and, in fact, is called to *support* the other.

I have talked with more than one divorced Christian. What I heard over and over again, if not literally, were the following words. These words are a wake-up call and of ultimate importance, at least on this plane.

"You know, Tony, if I knew then what I know now, I would have fought to the death to preserve my first marriage."

Deer Abbey Part 1

"If we make the basis of prayer our effort and agony and nights of prayer, we mistake the basis of prayer. The basis of prayer is not what it costs us, but what it cost God to enable us to pray."
—Oswald Chambers[62]

My black Lab, Abbey, and I went for our usual around-the-neighborhood walk at about 6:45 a.m. Friday morning, July 26. That morning when home, for the first time in forever, she didn't wolf down her breakfast. She ate it quickly enough, but Abbey is the type section (geologic terminology) most food-motivated dog on the planet. She normally, almost literally, jumps into her bowl of Bil-Jac. This morning, not so much. But, as the morning went on, she really slowed up and was obviously in pain. I have never, in all the years our family has had Abbey, even remotely seen her like this. There were times she would lie on her side with her eyes open and tail barely wagging, but I wasn't sure she was still here.

Calling our local vet, Animal Care Center in Panama City Beach, Florida, I made an appointment for that afternoon. She just wasn't herself. I think "lethargic" is the key term. At the vet she did perk up a bit, but that was because we were at the vet. When the doctor came in, Abbey tucked her tail so far under herself that it pretty well disappeared. She has *never* done this. She loves everybody, and, especially considering she is about nine-and-a-half years old, she remains something of a puppy. At times this can frustrate me but not anymore.

Our best guess was that she somehow injured her back. This would be a typical Lab injury at her age. After a full radiograph of her lungs, abdomen, and back (and tail), the Vet came in to discuss his findings with me. He told me essentially three things.

---

62 Chambers, O. (1938). *If ye shall ask. . . .* Grosset and Dunlap Publishers. http://prayermeetings.org/files/P_If_ye_shall_ask_Oswald_Chambers.pdf.

First, "I can't find anything wrong with Abbey." Second, "She has the skeletal system of a Lab two to three years old." That's great, but. . . the third thing, "We found a tumor in her right lung."

My heart sank, of course, but let's hear it. "Bad news, most likely a cancerous lung mass. Good news, it appears to be primary." At least he and the other doctors felt reasonably sure that the mass was not a product of metastasis, a spreading of the cancer from the primary sight. Where do we go from here?

Almost six years ago we took our other black Lab, Rhodie, to The Auburn University Veterinary Clinic at the Small Animal Teaching Hospital, Auburn, Alabama—about four hours north of where we live. They were fabulous and took great care of Rhodie. No, we are not really Beatles fans if you caught the Abbey-Rhodie thing. So, off we went to Auburn. They were terrific. Again. During the interview, I was asked to describe her initial symptoms, the reason for taking her to our local vet. After telling them the answer they seemed bewildered. I was told that this tumor doesn't present itself that way.

So, what was it then? We may never know, but I am certainly glad it happened. We caught this cancer early enough to do something about it. Without the Friday episode, we most likely would not have known it was there until it was too late. The doctors agree: when this type of lung cancer in dogs goes symptomatic, that commonly means game over. *Thank You, Lord.*

They took a CT Scan this time with various other tests, like simple blood work, looking for tumor markers. They agreed with the three local specialists—the tumor appeared primary, with no invasion of Abbey's lymph nodes and vascular system.

Of course, I was disappointed, having prayed and asked other friends and family members to pray for complete healing. I actually expected that the Lord would indeed remove the tumor and was looking forward to seeing the puzzled faces of the doctors as they wondered why we drove four hours for nothing. When we find ourselves face-to-face with disappointing news, we must recall that God is sovereign. He can be trusted in all things. We must yield, knowing full well that He loves us more than we will ever know. He removes tumors sometimes and leaves them in place at other times. He calms the storms sometimes, but sometimes He takes us by the hand and walks us through the storms. First faith, as in Luke 17:19, "Then he said to him, 'Rise and go; your faith has made you well.'" But we all know more than one wonderful and sincere Christian brother or sister who has been in and out of the hospital for a major portion of his or her life. So, faith is vital, but it is not the active agent in the medication. I am going to guess that the tumor disappears when the Lord knows that this miracle will bring Him more honor and glory, resulting in more people making it to the right side of eternity. If He allows the more common, natural progression—pain and trauma—then that will bring Him more honor and glory, resulting in more people making it to the right side of eternity. We cannot see or know. This is His territory. We have to trust Him.

In another essay, my next book perhaps, I plan to write up some thoughts as to how special animals are for the simple reason that zookeeper was our primary occupation—if only for a short time. Abbey is much more than my dog. She is the sweet soul that the Lord used to rescue me when I was facing the most difficult time in my life. Watching her do the simplest things, like running and jumping, warms my heart. She is a compassionate friend. Pet therapy deluxe. Deer—I mean... dear Abbey.

Tomorrow we leave for Auburn.

Carry On

"My main ambition in life is to be on the devil's most wanted list."
—Leonard Ravenhill[63]

"When you plead the name of Christ, you plead that which shakes the gates of hell and that which the hosts of heaven obey, and God Himself feels the sacred power of that divine plea."
—Charles Spurgeon[64]

Satan hates God and would very much like to dethrone Him and take over. He cannot. So, what is *Plan B*? Blind us, the apple of His eye, to the light of the gospel (2 Corinthians 4:4). What or whom does He love most? That's you, dear reader. Let us never forget that we are in the dark side's crosshairs every moment of every day, and be assured that the closer you move toward God, the greater the effort against you. 1 Peter 5:8 reads, "Be alert and of sober mind. Your enemy the devil prowls around like a roaring lion looking for someone to devour." Recall Job 1:7, "The LORD said to Satan, 'Where have you come from?' Satan answered the LORD, 'From roaming throughout the earth, going back and forth on it.'" In that regard, then, when your world seems to be unraveling, understand that it may be in a large part due to the simple fact that you are doing something right! You have gotten the enemy's attention. Christians who are not a threat are often allowed to continue living a comfortable but unprofitable life. If you are walking with the Lord, desiring Him, and all hell is breaking loose, rejoice! The dark side is in trouble, and knows it. Good for you. Carry on.

63 Pittman, A. (2013). *Equipped for Effectiveness in Spiritual Warfare.* Bridge-Logos Publishers.

64 Spurgeon, C. (1998). *Spurgeon on Prayer and Spiritual Warfare.* Whitaker House.

Check out James 4:7. "Submit yourselves, then, to God. Resist the devil, and he will flee from you." Also, 2 Thessalonians 3:3: "But the Lord is faithful, and he will strengthen you and protect you from the evil one."

How Should We Handle Panhandlers?

"Douglas recalls a story where Jack and a friend were walking to a meeting one day when they were approached by a beggar. The beggar asked them for some spare change whereupon Jack [C.S. Lewis] gave him everything he had. Once the beggar had gone, his friend said, 'You shouldn't have given that man all that money Jack, he'll only spend it on drink.' Jack's reply—'Well, if I'd kept it, I would have only spent it on drink.'"

—Stephen Liggins' interview with Douglas Gresham[65]

This is a tough topic. And one I usually have difficulty with: doing what I know the Lord wants me to do. Let's call it a sin of omission. First a short story, and then, well, another one.

Many years ago, when we lived in Katy, west of Houston, a gentleman approached the car as I was getting back in and told me the typical story. He lived in California. Was headed to the bus station to return home. Was robbed and now doesn't have the money to buy a ticket. Could I help? I reluctantly reached for my wallet and handed him some money, having no idea if that was the best thing to do.

Fast forward about a year. On and off, I had wondered what the Lord expected me to do. I have been accused of being Mr. Naïve (actually a preference to Mr. Cynical), but I did wonder if his story was anywhere close to being the truth. Panhandling or not, victim or not, telling the truth would be a better road to travel. Anyway, thinking about this on the way home after work one day, I prayed the following or something close to it.

"Lord, what did you want me to do about that guy that was asking for money a year ago? Should I have given him more?

65   Gresham, D. (1998). *According to the son* [Interview]. Anglican Media Sydney. https://cslewis.drzeus.net/papers/according-to-the-son/.

Less? Maybe I should have driven him to a restaurant or our local church. I don't know. He may have made it back home, wherever that is, though I suspect that was just the usual story." No "Amen." Just a short prayer asking for help to think through what happened, what could have happened, and possibly how to do better next time. Just then, after turning down one of the major roads near our neighborhood, I passed by the person of interest. It was definitely him. I hadn't seen him in a year. So, what were the chances of that happening? Near zero, of course. Another "I hear you" from the Lord. "Your friend is still here." This time he was hitchhiking. Maybe I should have turned around and helped him out. I just drove home.

I am going to guess we all struggle with this. But nothing is really that hard. We just try to figure out stuff on our own, rather than truly handing it off to the Lord. First step, most likely, is to pray about it. *Most likely? You think?* Pray about it. There may very well be times the Lord will nudge you into helping, whatever that means exactly, and there may very well be times he will send you "down the road" (pun intended). Be sensitive to His leading and desiring to do what He wants you to do. Of course, that is the remedy to every problem we face.

In the future, rather than crawling under the car seat, it would be best to make eye contact with the person. Hopefully, this in some way would convey compassion and a recognition that we see what they are experiencing. Driving a Lexus, it is obvious I do not understand what they are experiencing. I plan to put a bunch of my *Letters from Tony* books in the car someday, inserting a ten or twenty-dollar bill in each, and hand them out. Not my idea, His. Perhaps, all of us could buy some gift certificates to a local restaurant. Remember: "The generous will themselves be blessed, for they share their food with the poor" (Prov. 22:9), and, "Those who give to the poor will lack nothing, but those who close their eyes to them receive many curses." (Prov. 28:27)

One more thing. Back when I was in college, I would often take a train from Stamford, Connecticut, where my parents and girlfriend lived, to Grand Central Station in Manhattan. Then, I'd quickly run to the Port Authority. I was frequently at the bus station at night and, many times, quite late at night. You know, when all the police "go home." It didn't take me long to figure out that the little, scrawny college kid had better learn how to strike up a conversation with some of the big guys who lived at the Port Authority. This was about ten years before I accepted Christ, so understand my perspective. At that point, I was very capable of selfishly using people when it benefited me.

This is what I learned. Surprisingly, the overwhelming majority of the guys who were homeless and stayed in the Port Authority for shelter were not lazy or of modest intellect or lacked drive. Almost everyone I talked to, at one time, had a good job, a family, good health, and a home. Then, something tragic happened. They lost their job or health or family. They were crushed and tried to recover and, for various reasons, could not. My heart, more so now, goes out to these people. I am sure, given what is happening today, this ministry opportunity hasn't gone away.

Now I know there are only two kinds of people in this world, and the categories are not "being in a home" and "homeless." My heart still aches when I think of the men I met, and, if I was a Christian then, what I could have told them. I can't change that now, but I can change how I react to the panhandlers and the homeless in the future. You can, too.

Keeping Busy? Part 1

"If you have not the time, God gave it to you, and you must have misspent it."
—Charles Spurgeon[66]

What a dumb question: Are you keeping busy?

"Man, I am overloaded. Working my tail off. In fact, I work thirty-six hours each day. No time for anything. My wife's gone back to college, taking eighteen credit hours a semester. She is on the school board and volunteers at our church each morning. Kids are in basketball, baseball, volleyball, football, square dancing, tap, ballet, piano lessons, guitar lessons, and they see a college prep tutor after school."

(The kids are eleven and six years old.)

One way or the other in our casual greetings or the spoken (realized) or unspoken (sub-conscience), many people in our culture live at a crazy pace. The proliferation of smart phones (*chuckle*) and apps, such as Twitter and Facebook, keep us connected and reporting to someone, somewhere, constantly. Why do we insist on living this way, chasing after things we will never catch? If we did, we would find out quickly they weren't worth the effort. We miss so much.

From a Christian perspective, this is particularly foolish. The Christian life, in many ways, is quite simple. Look up. Period. Focus on Him. The Lord has given us twenty-four hours each and every day, exactly enough time to do everything He would have us accomplish. This is all the time we need. We need to stop cramming thirty-six hours of activity into the twenty-four hours we are given, and recalculate, restack, and learn to say, "No." I ask people occasionally, "How many hours a day do you spend reading the Bible?" You see: that's a front-end, loaded, accusatory challenge. Response? "Well, I am not retired like you,

66   Spurgeon, C. (1864). *A bad excuse is worse than none*. Spurgeon Gems. https://www.spurgeongems.org/sermon/chs578.pdf.

Carvalho." My terribly dry, geo-engineering response usually goes, "You sleep seven hours, eat for two, work about nine. So, what do you do with the other six?"

You see where I am headed. Haven't met a Christian yet that denied the importance and priority of spending time with Him, being in His presence, and enjoying His company. That means a daily combination of Scripture and prayer, preferably early in the morning before you get to your chore list. Follow Christ's example: "Very early in the morning, while it was still dark, Jesus got up, left the house and went off to a solitary place, where he prayed" (Mark 1:35). If this was important to Jesus, how much more should it be to us?

We can whittle down the six hours "left over" with many healthy activities, such as commitments to family or working out, but we all have at least a couple hours to do the most important things—Scripture and prayer. There is no excuse. The payoff in doing this, as simple as it is, is enormous. So, where does that leave us?

If you have too much to do, you are doing too much.

If not two hours, how about one?

Keeping Busy? Part 2

"The weight of so many responsibilities and distractions—even the worthwhile ones—has a crushing effect on a person's relationship with Christ."
—John MacArthur[67]

In our complex world we are inundated with stuff, much of it being entirely unnecessary. I am not a minimalist, but those people are definitely on to something. In this regard, one of the most important bottom-line Scriptures, especially given our culture, is the story of Martha and Mary. Martha has Jesus over. The living room is probably packed, standing room only (except for Mary, of course). And the story goes, "As Jesus and his disciples were on their way, he came to a village where a woman named Martha opened her home to him. She had a sister called Mary, who sat at the Lord's feet listening to what He said. But Martha was distracted by all the preparations that had to be made. She came to him and asked, 'Lord, don't you care that my sister has left me to do the work by myself? Tell her to help me'" (Luke 10:38-40)!

Poor Martha is slaving over a hot stove, turning out broiled Galilean Tilapia as fast as she can. People in her home are wondering why it is taking so long to get a light lunch. Martha's had it and most likely barges into the living room where Jesus is teaching their guests. She needs help in the kitchen. Now!

If I recall correctly, Jesus apologizes to her and tells Mary to get up and go help her sister. Or not: "'Martha, Martha,' the Lord answered, 'you are worried and upset about many things, but few things are needed—or indeed only one. Mary has chosen what is better, and it will not be taken away from her'" (Luke 10:41-42).

Yes, I am prone to exaggeration and hyperbole (sometimes

67   MacArthur, J. (2004). *Grace to you letter.* Grace To You.

in the same thought), but, please, focus on the scene. This is critical to our understanding—the solution for so much that plagues us. It may be that one of the greatest sins of the twenty-first century Church (believers) is simply *busyness.* We are too distracted. What does God want us to do? What does He expect? The answer is quite simple, especially in this case. Martha, as is true with each one of us, is trying to do too much and take care of too many things and too many people. Because she cannot, she becomes anxious, fretful, unsettled, and overwhelmed. She is distracted. She has Jesus at their house! And she is worried about serving her guests? Does this sound familiar? Forget all that stuff. Jesus reminds her (us) that *only one thing is needed.* When God tells us *only one thing is needed,* we really need to stop and listen. What was Mary's better choice? What was she doing to win such praise from our Lord? Key words in verse 39:

- Sat (she is sitting—not standing, running, or sweating)
- At the Lord's feet (not *with* or *in an equal posture* but at his feet humbled and adoring Him like a student before a Rabbi)
- Listening to (not debating with)
- What He said (His teaching, Word, Scripture)

How do we play Mary today? Sit and pray earnestly, asking the Spirit for His help. Listen to and/or read the Bible. Simple.

Porch Time

"Visit many good books, but live in the Bible."
—Charles Spurgeon[68]

Each and every morning, regardless of where I am, I spend the first two or three hours with a Bible in my hands. The "Hermit of Rosemary Beach" or "Monk of Rosemary," depending on the day and my mood, is usually at home, which is also the International Headquarters of Lehigh Ministries. Sounded rather weighty, didn't it? The home office literally measures seven by eleven, enough room for me and my laptop.

When at the house, the alarm goes off about 6:30 a.m. This is nothing as high-tech as an iPhone. Abbey, my black Lab, shakes her head—her slapping ears wake me up. This is her way of saying, "Hey Dad. Time to hit the trails." We go for our morning walk, come back, do the usual, then hit the porch. I have creatively called this time, "Porch Time." Abbey, *caw*fee, my two buddies Oswald and Charlie, and, of course, the Bible. Yes, I am retired so I can devote most every morning to this activity. That being said, I find that—even though I have lost the morning to writing and/or emailing and/or meeting with people—somehow, dedicating these first few hours of the day to Him assures the highest productivity in the remainder of the day. You cannot out give God.

Even when I travel, I do my best to set aside at least a portion of the morning to Porch Time. This is not a chore, nor do I feel that, if I somehow miss the appointment, the skies will open—revealing a disappointed Heavenly Father. Not at all. I truly desire, with all my heart, to do this. Like breathing or drinking water, I am not certain how to live without it.

Here is a danger. I really enjoy reading the daily devotionals and certain other works by Chambers and Spurgeon. I can

68   Roberts, J.A. (2020). *The conclusion*. J.A. Roberts. https://books.google.com/ books?id=1_PwDwAAQBAJ&dq=%E2%80%9C.

easily put my head into their work, as elegant and insightful as anything published, at the expense of spending time with other guys, such as Daniel, Paul, and Peter. But knowing the problem is the first step to solving it, so my use of the term "danger" was somewhat exaggerated. We are all called to live intentionally. Our weaknesses, if we are listening, require only gentle reminders guided by the Spirit to adjust. This means putting Oswald and Charlie "in their places" and picking up the Bible. Spending our moments with the Lord directly and hearing His voice will always be a higher calling as compared to reading "about" Him. No matter how astute the filter, it is still a filter. No matter how anointed, enabled, or led by the Spirit, it is not written by the Spirit. Please, don't misunderstand me. You cannot make a better choice in the "world of men" than Chambers and Spurgeon or more modern writers such as Sproul and Lewis.

Most of you cannot spend the morning on the porch or wherever your "porch" may be. But you can start your day with the Lord. Set the alarm or ask your puppy to shake his or her head. . . an hour earlier.

The Natives
Have Taken Over

"Prayer is the battle; it is a matter of indifference where you
are. Whichever way God engineers circumstances, the duty
is to pray."
—Oswald Chambers[69]

It was our second time to live in a Houston suburb. We bought
a new house. In fact, since we had only been gone a year, we
had the same builder build essentially the same home—in the
same neighborhood—to minimize the disruption to the family.
Oil companies are more than capable of imitating the service
when it comes to frequent transfers.

Here was one of the head-scratchers. Being Houston, there
was *plenty* of humidity and warmth. So, you would think
most plants would thrive easily, and the only thing the owner
or landscaping company would need is pruning shears. But
everything grows, even powdery mildew (a fungus), black spot,
petal blight, and root rot. Plants that just arrived at the nursery
down the street may come from anywhere in the U.S., so they
may not necessarily enjoy the Houston sauna. So, we planted
new plants and, even with the proper care (sprinklers in the
right place sprinkling at the right time, various root stimulators
carefully applied, root balls not buried or sometimes buried),
we ended up with plants that continued to struggle.

We eventually made the decision to dig the stuff up and start
over. How about we plant natives? Wow, what a concept. Let's
plant Red Turk's Cap, Texas Lantana (local flowering plants), and
native perennial grass, which grows easily in these soils and in
this climate. We started digging (not literally) but doing research
on the possibilities. After some hesitancy (native plants look

69   Chambers, O. (2017). *My Utmost for His Highest: Classic Edition* (3rd ed.). Our
Daily Bread Publishing.

like weeds because they essentially are) we decided to go for it! When the landscape plan was agreed to, we made it happen and then stood back and thought that, perhaps, the second try might have been a step backwards. Not bad, just something you might see driving west on I-10 or in the vacant lot across the street. Again, no real surprises. But seeing it in person—in *your* front yard—somehow spoke with a different accent than the photos in the magazines written by those who were more, let us just say, enthusiastic.

But relatively soon, here we go again: Uprooted (we are not talking landscaping) the family and headed north to Plano, a suburb of Dallas. Again. Yes, we used to live in Plano.

I was still traveling to Houston on business, so about a year or so later I decided to see the old neighborhood and drive by our previous home. *Oh my gosh!* The front yard was gorgeous. Spectacular in fact. The natives had taken over. They were healthy, flowering, and beautiful.

Lesson learned? Instead of force fitting the plants from the West Coast or wherever, consider planting the ones that are intended for the area. And add a good dose of patience.

Much more importantly: instead of fighting with the Lord as to what you do and where you do it, blend into His landscape. No, the grass is not greener on the other side of the fence. Not everything He does or wants us to do can be called common sense. Sometimes we are certainly called to step out of our comfort zone. But if it is in our hearts to simply please Him wherever we are planted, we will be hugely successful. Also consider, the native plants required virtually no upkeep. The natives naturally enjoyed the rain, warmth, and soil. That's where they were meant to be. Wherever the Lord puts you is *exactly* where you are meant to be. You are a native plant.

Let's agree with Paul as he tells us in Philippians chapter 4 verse 11: "I have learned to be content whatever the circumstances."

What Do You Bother God about?

"We have to pray with our eyes on God, not on our difficulties."
—Oswald Chambers[70]

One day at Bible Study I asked everybody, "So, what do you bother God about?" In other words, I was simply asking, "In the supplication portion of your prayers, what do you commonly ask for?" First responders gave the usual "heavy" list, such as peace, healing, and job security. You know—the God things. A number of the attendees were calmly holding back, but even a brief glance at their body language assured me of an energetic rebuttal. So, igniting the kindling, I just looked around with a casual expression meaning "anybody else?"

Boom!

"Are you kidding? How about a bad-hair day or where the heck are my car keys?"

Over the years I have heard various versions of the same comments. Some people believe you only "bother" God with God things—the stuff only He can handle because, apparently, we can handle the rest. Others have this idea that we can put anything (literally anything) in our prayers.

Realized or not, we really can't do much on our own, so, of course, we should ask Him for help in all things. God is Sustainer and is intimately involved in everything, so this makes sense. Also, we like to think we are very capable, but in fact we are not. A childlike faith should result in the kids seeking Dad's advice, help, and provision for *everything*. Dad's in a much better position to get the job done than we are. The concept of co-laboring with the Lord remains intact, but the realization that He does the

70   Chambers, O. (2008). *The Quotable Oswald Chambers* (David McCasland, Ed.). Discovery House Publishing.

heavy lifting must be retained. It is true that God does make it possible for us to do *all* things—everything that He wants us to do (Phil. 4:13). But the fact that our hearts are not beating by themselves is also perhaps a good reminder of how much we need God involved—in everything. First Peter 5:7 reads, "Cast all your anxiety on him because he cares for you." The last time I checked, the Greek word rendered *all* means *all*.

Think Big,
No Bigger, Bigger

"Never allow the thought—'I am of no use where I am'; because you certainly can be of no use where you are not."
—Oswald Chambers[71]

"God is able to use your life for future purposes you cannot imagine today."
—Jim Denison[72]

I am not particularly a Simpsons fan, but I do appreciate some segments, especially those that remind me of what is most important. In one episode (Stern, 1990), Otto (the bus driver) and Bart have an amusing and somewhat insightful exchange:

OTTO: Ah! So, what's in your head, little man?
BART: Well, I've been failing a lot of tests recently.
OTTO: Yeah-huh.
BART: And now they're talkin' about holding me back in the fourth grade if I don't shape up.
OTTO: That's it? Hey, relax, man! It could end up being the best thing that ever happened to ya. I got held back in the fourth grade myself. Twice! Look at me, man! Now I drive the school bus![73]

Another day at the office. My primary tasks at work became

71 Chambers, O. (2017). *My Utmost for His Highest: Classic Edition* (3rd ed.). Our Daily Bread Publishing.

72 Denison, J. (2017, May 4). Student ordered to leave class for reading Bible. *Denison Forum*. Retrieved March 17, 2021 from https://www.denisonforum.org/columns/daily-article/student-ordered-leave-class-reading-bible/.

73 Stern, D. M. (Writer), & Silverman, D. (Director). (1990). Bart gets an "f" [Television series episode]. In J. L. Brooks (Producer), The Simpsons. Culver City, CA: Gracie Films 20th Television.

strained negotiations with a sister division as to who commits the millions of dollars to delineate a field in the Gulf of Mexico and whom to lay off. Many people believe that the Petroleum Industry has been rolling in the money and generating huge profits ever since oil was created, but that is simply not the case. It seemed like we were having layoffs constantly, and, most times, they were deep. Sometimes literally fifty percent of the *remaining* staff. When your primary job description or title becomes Master-Arm-Twister and Forced-Rank-Then-Fire guy, you know you're not having a lot of fun.

The experience with a major gave me the exact "skills" needed to participate in the early days of the shale revolution. Learning what to do and, in many ways, what not to do was invaluable. On my current chore list (not quite at the top) is to instigate the writing of a book. Novel idea (pun intended). But this would be one entitled, "7-7-7: The True Story Behind Chief Oil & Gas."

Here's my point for this essay. All that banging my head against a brick wall more than paid off. If you find yourself in a dead-end job, please just pray about it. Don't automatically jump ship and pursue some elusive dream that God never intended. Take each step being fully aware of the Holy Spirit's leading. Sometimes He will say, "Quit and move on." Sometimes He will say, "Stay put. Grin and bear it." We would never ever, on our own, be able to tell the difference. It doesn't matter how smart or well-intentioned you are. The Lord's purposes may not have the look and feel of "common sense." "Trust in the LORD," as Solomon writes in Proverbs 3:5-6, "with all your heart and lean not on your own understanding; in all your ways submit to him, and he will make your paths straight."

But seven years, seven deals, seven billion dollars? You see the Lord's fingerprints all over that success story. We co-labored, but the Lord did the heavy lifting. The Triple Seven (for emphasis) is a clear message designed by the Lord to indicate the idea of completeness and perfection. Recall Joshua's conquest of Jericho. "On the seventh day, they got up at daybreak and marched around the city seven times in the same manner, except that on that day they circled the city seven times" (Josh. 6:15). Also consider Matthew 18:21-22, "Then Peter came to Jesus and asked, 'Lord, how many times shall I forgive my brother or sister who sins against me? Up to seven times?' Jesus answered, 'I tell you, not seven times, but seventy-seven times.'" I doubt Jesus was telling Peter (and us) to keep a record of how many times we forgive someone. His answer, using more than one seven, expresses the fullness of the command to forgive completely. Don't leave the door partially open. Always (completely) forgive and don't stop.

We need to proceed down the path of "biblical numerology" with caution due to the abuse inflicted over the years. The concept has been extrapolated into many areas most likely never intended by the Lord. A search on Google would suggest we can use the notion as a tool of magic or a secret door into a hidden passageway similar to fortune telling. "When is your birthday? February 15? Okay, on your birthday, the second month and fifteenth day, look at Mark chapter 2 verse 15 at 2:15 p.m. And, then, do what it says."

Uh-oh. Sounds dangerous, but not for this guy. I hope he has a good friend named Levi. Obviously, I am exaggerating (at your expense) to make a point. However, the numerous occurrences of seven (and also six, ten, twelve and forty), many conservative biblical scholars believe, are meaningful and intentional.

And *no one* saw the Chief Story coming. Meaning: some of the very best things in life will not be anticipated. The things we see ahead are usually a result of our "human" planning. The things that get dropped in our laps are, at least more obviously, choreographed from above. "Every good and perfect gift is from above," reads James 1:17, "coming down from the Father of the heavenly lights, who does not change like shifting shadows."

So, now what? The 7-7-7 accomplishment is going to be a bit difficult to top. You think? But, actually, if we truly believe that all things worth doing or having come from our Lord, then why do we insist on limiting God? I often pray, "Lord, let the Chief Oil & Gas outcome be like warming up in the bull pen. Now, we're ready to pitch in the World Series!"

This should be the mindset of each one of us who trust Christ with our lives. And, please, don't misunderstand me. True, this essay is about a financial success story, but I am not talking about what is generally referred to today as the "prosperity gospel." The "World Series" can be ministry work, career opportunities, knowledge, wisdom, or relationships built or strengthened. It can also be the most valuable: a much closer walk with the Lord. What's that worth? Everything.

Hang in there, no matter where the Lord puts you. Experience with a *thankful* heart all that He sends your way. Be salt and light. One day, soon, you will "drive the school bus"!

The Calgarian Visitor

"The angels must often be astonished at us and think we are the strangest creatures that well can be, yet they love us, and therefore they take a great interest in that Gospel that promotes our highest good."
—Charles Spurgeon[74]

A few years ago, I was in Calgary on a business trip and staying at a hotel downtown. One morning I decided to go for a walk with the intent of finding somewhere to eat a late breakfast. The hotel restaurant had stopped serving, and, besides, seeing more of downtown Calgary sounded like a good idea. I cannot recall the exact date, but it was during the time of shorter days and longer nights and was cold. Very cold. The previous night's low was below zero. That morning it had warmed up to about zero. Walking through a very quiet part of the city mid-morning with all office buildings, nothing seemed to be moving, and, given the extreme cold, that seemed appropriate. There were very few people out and about. I did see someone—a homeless person sitting on the sidewalk near a major intersection, hunched over, and covered only with what looked like a finely woven burlap or canvas material. I asked if he (she?) was all right. My first dumb question of the encounter. I was prepared to meet an individual who was unshaven, obviously homeless, destitute, in need in so many ways, and, perhaps, in poor health. After a couple attempts to get his attention, he finally lifted his head and removed the fabric just enough to uncover his face and top of his chest (the fabric still being over his head like a hood). I was shocked. Long blonde hair, deep-blue penetrating and translucent eyes, perhaps about thirty years old. He had perfect facial features and absolutely no facial hair. I am not accustomed to using this term when it comes to a guy, but it fits in this case. He was

74   Spurgeon, C. (1870). *A String of Pearls.* Precept Austin. https://www.preceptaustin.org/sermons_by_spurgeon_-_1_peter_1.

beautiful. Nobody looks like this, especially compared to my expectations of this poor soul sitting on a sidewalk in downtown Calgary in the cold!

We talked for a while. Actually, I talked he listened. Tried my best to convince him that we should go to a restaurant—better perhaps, a clothing store to buy him a down vest or coat. He just looked at me with what I can only recall as subtle amusement. I was getting frustrated, so I said something thoroughly ridiculous like, "I am a Christian. I have to do something. I want to help you." He looked up at me offering a slight grin and said, "I am a. . . Christian too." There was a definite pause before he admitted to being a Christian, and his grin became a bit more pronounced. This struck me as being odd. He seemed to know something I didn't. Again, he seemed somewhat amused. More debate (one direction) then I finally gave up.

Before freezing solid I decided to take off, walking about as fast as I could. Must have walked no more than fifty feet, which probably took about five seconds. My failure haunted me, so I turned abruptly to give it one more try. One problem: He was gone. Assuming he got up as soon as I left and ran down one direction of the cross street, I hustled back to the intersection even quicker than I had walked away. A modest jog. Got to the corner, looked to the right and left. No one. Completely gone.

It wasn't until days later that I began to understand that this was no ordinary guy. Not only did he have beautiful features and apparently could easily withstand the cold; he had literally disappeared. His reaction to my comment and his agreement that he, too, was a *hesitation, smile,* "Christian," was very odd. One more thing: I was absolutely sure that this guy could easily level Calgary if need be. Don't ask me how I knew that. I just knew it. There is little doubt in my mind that this brief encounter was with a ministering spirit (Heb. 1:14).

Please, understand I am not the type to expect this kind of experience in my Christian walk. Some odd things have happened to me (not a lot), but this was certainly one. It is always, *always,* necessary to thoroughly search and examine Scripture to see if a conflict might exist between the only source of non-negotiable, ultimate truth (canon) and what we experience. Certainly, the overwhelming majority of weird spiritual experiences that occur in today's world are sourced by the dark side and not from God. Pretty simple. I even hesitate telling this story for obvious reasons, but I strongly—more important, prayerfully—believe that there are references in Scripture that allow for this kind of interaction. One of the clearest (if not the clearest), especially given this situation, is Hebrews 13:2. "Do not forget to show hospitality to strangers, for by so doing some people have shown hospitality to angels without knowing it."

For years this had been my dilemma: "Why Lord? Why the heck did this happen? I didn't need help. Did I need to know something?" Better, what did the Lord want me to do or say? Was this simply a test that, perhaps, I failed? You can see my perspective, and I believe the perspective of many Christians is to automatically assume we are being tested. Is it about performance? Obedience? You see my confusion. I wanted to do more, but I didn't know what to do or say. It's kind of funny, actually. What could I have done to help this guy anyway? Buy him breakfast? How about a down vest?

Many years later, when I was feeling particularly down (pun intended) and dealing with a reasonably serious, personal difficulty, the Lord interrupted my whining and feeling sorry for myself with a subtle reminder of this northern experience. Again, stuck in a rut, I dropped back into the same thought pattern: *More failure. More questions.* That was the last thing I needed, especially at that moment. *Pile it on.* I was being reminded that I failed and lost again. But here is the terrific part of the story. The *silent ceiling* (yes, never received an answer to my questions over all those years), finally opened up with a very clear and direct answer. I call these thoughts or answers to prayer Triple A's (Almost An Audible).

> *Tony, I didn't want you to do or say anything. I wasn't testing you. I know your heart. This was done then to better show you today that I love you. I am intimately involved in everything you do. You will get through what you are facing today. I sent my messenger as a gentle reminder that you are loved and nothing will ever happen to you that I do not allow.*

Now, the above was not verbatim. I cannot recall exactly what the Lord dropped on me that day, but clearly the message was of that kind. Meeting "The Calgarian Visitor" was simply His way of letting me know (years in advance of when I needed it most) that I was loved, cared for in every way, and protected. Please, understand that this is the heart of the Lord we worship. Stop trying to prove your worth. Stop feeling like a failure and open yourself up to the One who loves you unconditionally. Carry on and do great things in His power and His strength because you love Him. Again, pretty simple.

These verses remind us of His steadfast love and protection:

> Have I not commanded you? Be strong and courageous. Do not be afraid; do not be discouraged, for the LORD your God will be with you wherever you go.
> (Josh. 1:9)

> Even though I walk through the darkest valley, I will fear no evil, for you are with me; your rod and your staff, they comfort me.
> (Ps. 23:4)

> The LORD is my light and my salvation, whom shall I fear? The LORD is the stronghold of my life of whom shall I be afraid?
> (Ps. 27: 1)

> Where can I go from your Spirit? Where can I flee from your presence?
> (Ps. 139:7)

> The LORD appeared to us in the past saying: "I have loved you with an everlasting love; I have drawn you with unfailing kindness."
> (Jer. 31:3)

AFTERTHOUGHT: It may have also been, in addition to the lesson learned years later, that I was headed toward a situation that the

Lord sent "The Calgarian Visitor" to prevent. Perhaps, in my walking around downtown Calgary, I would have foolishly stepped off the curb and gotten clobbered by a rapid, articulated transit bus. It may have not been my time, and this accident was choreographed by the dark side. Our brief conversation may have changed the appointment. I guess I will never know until the other side of the river, and, of course, at that point it won't matter.

PART FOUR:

Winning Each Day No Matter the Score

Should We Integrate Faith and Life?

"I understand that I am a Christian first and a congressman second. My faith is not divorced from my life."
—Tim Walberg[75]

"I believe in Christianity as I believe that the sun has risen: not only because I see it, but because by it I see everything else."
—C.S. Lewis[76]

"Should we fully integrate faith and every aspect of our existence? Should our personal Christian worldview be the prism through which all of our life decisions are made? In this increasingly secular and politically correct culture, how is it possible to put Christ at the fore? If we do that, won't we alienate people at work? People on the basketball team? At the restaurant?"

There are many Christians, I would guess (only a guess) the majority of evangelicals, who may declare a belief that it is best to include God in everything but in practice do not—a classic "plan vs. execution" dilemma. What seems appropriate, if not honestly and internally agreed to, will fall by the wayside quite easily, in fact: as soon as it becomes uncomfortable to do what a Christian ought to do or to say what a Christian ought to say. Put another way, we give a casual nod to ethics (oughtness, what should be) when, in actuality, the sport we play is morality

75   *Do no harm: Examining the misapplication of the 'religious freedom and restoration act': Hearing before the Committee on Education and Labor U.S. House of Representatives, 116th Congress. (2019). https://www.congress.gov/event/116th-congress/house-event/LC65209/text?s=1&r=1.*

76   Lewis, C.S. (1962). *They asked for a paper.* Samizdat University Press. http://www.samizdat.qc.ca/arts/lit/Theology=Poetry_CSL.pdf.

(isness, what is). What is—what we find ourselves immersed in at any particular time and place—becomes the stage where we decide on the fly which rules are to be followed. It is much easier to mirror the situation we find ourselves in rather than stand out. Many times, blending into our culture, to the natural man, is the safest option. Peace trumps righteousness to the natural man. We're not natural. Not anymore.

We must be led by the Spirit each moment of every day, not simply when we hang out together on Sunday mornings from 10 a.m. to 12 p.m. In fact, those are the times we should let the real us—blood, guts, and feathers if need be—surface. The fact that Sunday morning praise and worship services can be reduced to dress-up-and-smile time suggests a focus on worldly passions—not the One we are most passionate about. Sunday mornings and Wednesday evenings are times for the spiritual hospitals to be open for business.

If we love the world, we are doing something wrong. Consider 1 John 2:15: "Do not love the world or anything in the world. If anyone loves the world, love for the Father is not in them." Dear reader, please, understand that I am not suggesting we jump into the car each day in full anticipation of picking a fight with those we will see. But our jobs, "Ambassadors for Christ" and "Representatives of the Kingdom," are full-time positions. The Lord did not say, "Go. Wait. . . go when you get a few minutes." Our sole purpose, the reason we are here, is not to engage in a casual or part-time occupation. We are to walk with our Lord each minute of every day no matter what happens.

Negotiating is difficult. Trying to decide when to do or not do something necessitates an internal struggle. Being always engaged in living for Him is actually quite simple, assuming a heart that is truly yielded, contrite, and—as our friend Oswald Chambers often says—abandoned. No negotiating. No questions. Done. Period.

Delta Force Jesus

"For the believer there is hope beyond the grave, because Jesus Christ has opened the door to heaven for us by His death and resurrection."
—Billy Graham[77]

Let's imagine we are headed to a major foreign city and get redirected to Damascus instead. Numerous terrorists take over the plane, shouting orders at the passengers. This intensely frightening event seems to last forever, but the plane finally lands. Immediately, special forces surround the jet and break into the interior cabin. Imagine now you somehow manage to secure a weapon. Whom would you shoot?

Nearly two thousand years ago, the second person of the Trinity went on a rescue mission. He entered into time and space to free us from the adversary's control and to give us a way to avoid a bad ending that actually would never end. As it turns out, we participated in killing the special ops soldier sent our way. Does this make any sense at all? I understand that Jesus was born to die, and we would not have been rescued if Christ did not suffer actual death. The metaphor breaks down in many ways quickly. My purpose in suggesting we contemplate the ridiculous is simply to say that, given a situation where we were being rescued, we would obviously never do anything to make it more difficult or dangerous for the one sent to save us. But, as it turned out, we all participated in doing just that nearly two thousand years ago.

77   Graham, B. (2016, Mar. 23). 5 verses on hope found in Jesus Christ. *Billy Graham Library.* https://billygrahamlibrary.org/5-verses-on-hope-found-in-jesus-christ/.

Do You Have
a Bucket List?

"Aim at Heaven and you will get Earth 'thrown in': aim at
Earth and you will get neither."
—C.S. Lewis[78]

If so, why? As we get older, spending extra time with friends
and relatives can make a huge difference, especially to an
elderly person. If the motive behind the list and the particular
destinations to visit before passing away is to spend special time
with those who will be left behind, terrific. Creating memories
to hold on to is a wise investment. Focusing on spending our
remaining years playing catch up or doing the things we longed to
do but never did? Not so much. The Christian will spend eternity
in paradise, a Garden of Eden of sorts, in the full, loving, face-
to-face relationship with our Lord. Help me understand, why
our "retirement" years (and then our remaining years) should
be spent chasing what *this* world has to offer.

Our final destination will make anything in this world look
cheap, pale, unreal, counterfeit. Heaven may look a lot like
earth but in so many ways greater, deeper, more brilliant, richer.
Chasing the bucket list to taste the insignificant while heading
toward the significant is difficult to justify.

What might be a better use of our time is simply to focus our
remaining years here, sharing our faith in word and, certainly,
by the way we walk. Pleading—imploring if necessary. Someone
said, "passionately persuading." Bringing our friends and
relatives to Glacier National Park, Vancouver, or Paris may
sound exciting. Bringing them to heaven will be so much more.

I used to have a bucket list. I tossed it out a while back and
now spend my time with Abbey, my black Lab, doing various

78   Lewis, C.S. (2001). *Mere Christianity*. HarperCollins Publishers (Original work
published 1952).

ministry-related things like writing books. But being a geologist and never visiting the Grand Canyon? That may be hard to explain someday.

God Will Pick the Nut

"But we are so gentle and quiet, we do not use strong language about other people's opinions; but let men go to hell out of charity to them."
—Charles Spurgeon[79]

I was attending a National AAPG convention in San Antonio. The year was 1989. You can only sit still listening to someone talk about doing research on rocks for so long, so one afternoon I gave up and went for a stroll downtown. I was walking past the Alamo and came up to a guy literally standing on, well, let's call it a soap box while holding a Bible in his left hand, waving fiercely with his right, and warning the crowd in a very direct way that unless they repented they would spend eternity in hell. I reacted as I suppose most well-meaning Christians would have by quickly crossing the street, walking past the Alamo and the preacher, and, then, crossing back to my original path. I found myself shaking my head over what had just occurred. My response? A casual prayer, almost an apology, for a crazy Christian who should know better.

Fast forward about thirty years. What do I make of this encounter now? Conservative Biblical Christians (emphasis on the word *Biblical*) may collectively wince at the thought of being so straightforward. Certainly, I believe that an approach to bringing people to Christ that emphasizes the loving, sacrificial, and patient heart of our Lord is a better method, but here is the problem: I often think, at least initially, in bookends or extreme cases that bracket the problem, knowing full well that many times it is a better solution to strike a balance—something of a combination of various aspects or elements of the extreme cases.

79 Spurgeon, C. (1869). *The former and the latter rain.* The Spurgeon Center for Biblical Preaching at Midwestern Seminary. https://www.spurgeon.org/resource-library/sermons/the-former-and-the-latter-rain/#flipbook/.

Okay, I get it.

But we have gone overboard. Desiring to not offend, we have erred on the culturally correct, peaceful, gentle, and accepting side. In other words—thou shalt not judge. Apparently, our modern-day culture now defines love as the pursuit of a peaceful feeling. Gone are the days of "Tough Love." Put another way, Jesus has become all Lamb and no Lion. We have lost the basic definition of what it means to be a Christian. Yes, self-sacrificing, turning the cheek, and, sure, getting stepped on—who cares? But we must offer the truth no matter how it is received or how much it is shunned and out of favor. Universalism reigns supreme, but that is not God's Way. His Way is through a narrow gate. If we think the Lord is being too restrictive and quite closed-minded, we do not understand the radical uniqueness of Christ. He alone was and is the God-Man. Period. The End. Full Stop.

Jesus has done everything for us—everything we could ever desire. If that doesn't sound right (true), please, immerse yourself in Scripture and don't come up for air until you understand the words spoken to you in the love letter—what we call the Bible.

Is there a heaven? Is there a hell? The San Antonio gentleman (okay, a bit direct with his non-negotiable warning) was at least getting to the bottom line: the truth. There are only two kinds of people in this world. Those taking a right turn at eternity's door and those taking a left.

Do you know how many of our dear friends and relatives will experience the Lord's eternal judgement and wrath? See how I lightened up the reference? There is little doubt in my mind that, if God looked down on San Antonio that day and saw the nut and then looked ahead and saw many of us in the church here in the US, there would be no contest. *God would pick the nut.*

It is time for us to move away from the grand acceptance of every *ism* (every wind of teaching) ever known and move with certainty toward the nut. No reason to be apologetic. Yes, loving, gentle, respectful, but direct. Let's get serious. It is a narrow path and a matter of life and death. As Paul writes, "Then we will no longer be infants, tossed back and forth by the waves, and blown here and there by every wind of teaching and by the cunning and craftiness of people in their deceitful scheming. Instead, speaking the truth in love, we will grow to become in every respect the mature body of him who is the head, that is, Christ" (Eph. 4:14-15).

And Peter as well: "But in your hearts revere Christ as Lord. Always be prepared to give an answer to everyone who asks you to give the reason for the hope that you have. But do this with gentleness and respect" (1 Peter 3:15).

I Just Don't Enjoy
Reading the Bible

"There is no cordial of comfort like that which is poured from the bottle of Scripture."
—Charles Spurgeon[80]

This is a common hurdle experienced by all Christians at one time or the other. I am not a psychologist, so no attempt will be made to understand the various causes of the ailment. I can only tell you what I did not too long ago, in fact, that has worked very, very well. Even though I led a Bible Study for years, I would have to admit that my desire to bury myself in Scripture was not at the pitch it is now. So, this is what I did.

Oops.

What I meant was this is how the Lord led me through the maze, so that, now, the times I spend with a Bible in my hand are by far the most enjoyable and important times of my day. As a good friend recently said when telling me about her relationship with Christ, "Tony, I can't get enough of Him."

Wow. Let's call this a healthy addiction.

Permit me a sidebar. We have heard it said, "All things in moderation." That's pretty good advice for nearly everything. Nearly. Getting to know the Lord, hearing His voice, praying, and reading Scripture are clearly exceptions. Total immersion may be a better way to go. I see this in some ways like drinking water. You can drink too much water. But how many people drink too much? By far the error is not drinking enough. While we are here, could you spend too much time with the Lord? I guess so, but this is hardly worth mentioning. If you spent all day reading the Bible and never spent any time with your spouse and kids and failed to show up to work, well, enough said. But

80   Spurgeon, C. (2014). *The Treasury of David: Classic Reflections on the Wisdom of the Psalms (Vol. 1)*. Hendrickson Publishers.

who would do that? Seriously.

Part of the transition from casual reading, study, and preparation with a Bible in hand to, "I could do this all day," was birthed by a very difficult situation in my life. Bottom line: my way of dealing with the pain was simply to pour myself out to Him. I needed to hear His voice. That meant reading the Psalms over and over again. But alongside the difficulties that we all experience was already a commitment that I was going to just "push my way through it." Again, I hear something of a sneaker commercial in my head, but it is a fact of life. Sometimes, it *ain't gonna* be easy. You just have to push your way through it.

I committed to myself and (more importantly) to the Lord that I would pursue His Word when I felt like it and when I didn't. I decided to jump in with everything I had. Sometimes that was with a lot of energy, and sometimes with a lot of forced effort. But, the more you chase God and His Word, the more He will draw you in. That's the critical component. When *we* try to do stuff independently of seeking Him, it usually backfires. Think New Year's resolutions.

Do you trust Him? Yes? Do you love Him? Does He love you? This stuff has to become, in your mind and heart, so much more than simple intellectual realizations. They must become a part of you. We all need to be retooled at times. This is like any training. Pick a sport or a musical instrument. Nobody became great by casually tossing a ball once in a while or strumming a guitar for fifteen minutes a day. This is commitment time. Immerse yourself. And don't stop until it is a part of you. Put yourself on autopilot, and, yes, it will become much less of a chore and much more of a joy.

In fact, I can now play "China Grove" by the Doobie Brothers! More or less. I'm no Doobie Brother, but at least you would recognize it if I played it for you. How did this very mediocre guitar player do that? Simple: I spent about six months (yes, six), online with a guitar instructor on YouTube. That was a pain. But that was my "Now I can die and go to heaven" accomplishment— at least the one with a Stratocaster.

I veered off, only reason being to make a point. You know every Christian needs to spend time—quality focused time and secret prayer-closet time praying and reading the Bible. Commit to doing it, and don't quit until it becomes a part of you.

One more thing: During the full-court press stage, every evening when I would hit the hay, I would log in to BibleGateway and allow our good friend, Max McLean, to read my favorite parts of Scripture. I used to listen to the Psalms every night when things got tough. Now, I bounce around. I find it enormously encouraging to wake up and immediately hear God's Word.

And relatively often, I have a dream prompted by a specific part of the Bible. Sometimes a dream that is quite alarming. An example might be that I am searching for a beautiful place that is perfectly peaceful, but I cannot find it, like Cain, "So the LORD God banished him from the Garden of Eden to work the ground from which he had been taken. After he drove the man out, he placed on the east side of the Garden of Eden cherubim and a flaming sword flashing back and forth to guard the way to the tree of life" (Gen 3:23-24).

Be careful, though, especially if you are a light sleeper. Certain portions of Scripture may wake you up with a jolt, as this verse did: "About three in the afternoon Jesus cried out in a loud voice, 'Eli, Eli, lema sabachthani?' (which means 'My God, my God, why have you forsaken me?')" (Matt. 27:46).

But, then, sometimes a wonderful dream. I have found the beautiful place that is perfectly peaceful, and it reminds of this promise: "No longer will there be any curse. The throne of God and of the Lamb will be in the city, and his servants will serve him. They will see his face, and his name will be on their foreheads. There will be no more night. They will not need the light of a lamp or the light of the sun, for the Lord God will give them light. And they will reign for ever and ever" (Rev. 22:3-5).

No More
Shoats and Geeps

"We shall soon be in a world in which a man may be howled down for saying that two and two make four, in which furious party cries will be raised against anybody who says that cows have horns, in which people will persecute the heresy of calling a triangle a three-sided figure, and hang a man for maddening a mob with the news that grass is green."
—G.K. Chesterton[81]

"Two things I ask of you, LORD; do not refuse me before I die: Keep falsehood and lies far from me; give me neither poverty nor riches."
—Agur ben Jakeh[82]

Not too long ago, I was whining to a good friend of mine who happens to be a pastor. It seemed to me that a significant portion of our society had moved well beyond the "simply mistaken" phase. It was now possible to be *entirely* wrong. The 180-problem.

"Tony," he replied, "I think what the Lord is doing is separating the sheeps from the goats." His Middle Eastern accent made the comment and insight even more engaging. It was his unnegotiable opinion that what we were seeing was exactly what we should expect.

The Lord gives us many opportunities to make the right decisions, but, often, a certain portion of the crowd will choose to follow not only the wrong path but the *opposite* path. "Woe to those who call evil good and good evil," as Isaiah 5:20-21 reads,

81   Chesterton, G.K. (1991). *The Collected Works of G. K. Chesterton, Vol. 34* (Lawrence J. Clipper, Ed.) Ignatius Press.
82   Proverbs 30:7-8

"who put darkness for light and light for darkness, who put bitter for sweet and sweet for bitter. Woe to those who are wise in their own eyes and clever in their own sight."

We know psychologists refer to a related malady called projection. An individual or group is capable of making accusations (sometimes wild accusations), suggesting with passionate vigor that the other team is not playing by the rules. The wilder the accusation, the more we should be alerted as to the possibility that we are witnessing projection and anticipate that the accuser is actually the one guilty of the alleged oversight or transgression. It took me forever to see this in my previous life in the Petroleum Industry or while investing, but I finally caught on. A partner, vendor, contractor, or employee would make a statement, giving us a warning and suggesting we beware of a certain issue. Then, we found out (many times too late) that they were the guilty party. The fallout in the business world can be costly and harm trust that was developed over years. But the real danger occurs when this game is played, and our faith is in the crosshairs. Now we see the potential for significant spiritual and eternal damage.

We may have to go all the way back to the 1950s, the last decade where a significant portion of the people living in the United States could be labeled *Shoats and Geeps*. Maybe "everybody" wasn't a Christian, regardless of what they claimed when phoned by Gallup. But Judeo-Christian principles were widely accepted as the best way to live, and a reasonable and honest attempt was made by most to "walk the talk." There were plenty of sheep and goats, but there were also *shoats and* geeps trying to bridge the divide, finding life more complicated than anticipated but doing "the best they could." Not as much so now.

The field is becoming more polarized, as appears to be the case in other arenas dealing with other issues. But all problems are essentially *spiritual* problems. Our sovereign Lord is relentlessly moving us forward eventually into a One-World Government led overwhelmingly by the spirit of the Anti-Christ. There will be on earth, as there will be on the other side, a clear divide.

Be a sheep. Not a goat:

"But if serving the LORD seems undesirable to you, then choose for yourselves this day whom you will serve, whether the gods your ancestors served beyond the Euphrates, or the gods of the Amorites, in whose land you are living. But as for me and my household, we will serve the LORD" (Josh. 24:15).

One of My Worst Nightmares

"Racism, white nationalism, and white supremacy all make no sense if you are a Christian. Christians literally worship a dark-skinned, Jewish savior from the Middle East. Not only is racism sinful, it is remarkably stupid for anyone who identifies as a Christian."
—Ed Stetzer[83]

"I refuse to accept the view that mankind is so tragically bound to the starless midnight of racism and war that the bright daybreak of peace and brotherhood can never become a reality… I believe that unarmed truth and unconditional love will have the final word."
—Martin Luther King[84]

Can you imagine a world where essentially everyone looks like you, talks like you, and believes what you believe? Haven't met anyone yet who thinks that would be great. Actually, my guess is most people would say that idea sounds like a "nightmare." A pretty scary one. Clearly, a world of "just-ourselves" would be really bad. If this is true, how could any of us entertain truly racist thoughts—or worse—practices? If so, we have stumbled upon another clear case of cognitive dissonance. Never a reasonable way to think going forward.

Of course, from a Christian perspective, there are only two

83   Stetzer, E. (2019, August 4). *Racism, white nationalism, and white supremacy all make no sense if you are a Christian. Christians literally worship a dark-skinned* [Status update]. Facebook. https://www.facebook.com/edstetzer/posts/10157466827105909?comment_id=10157467235270909.

84   King, M. L., Jr. (1964, December 10). *Acceptance address for the Nobel peace prize.* The Martin Luther King, Jr. Research and Education Institute of Stanford. https://kinginstitute.stanford.edu/king-papers/documents/acceptance-address-nobel-peace-prize.

kinds of people in this world. There are those who have been born and those who have been born again. Period. The two categories are not black or white, short or tall, smart or *perhaps-not-as-smart*, young or old, rich or poor. I could go on. These dividing lines do just that. They divide.

One of the best passages in the Bible for today was written by James. In chapter 2:1-13, he walks us through the sin of favoritism. For instance, are we to treat people differently depending on their wealth? No. Also, consider, we must be the same person twenty-four hours each day, regardless of what or whom we are dealing with. If we are indwelt by the Holy Spirit, we must treat people as Christ did. He was impressed neither with the leaders nor the rich guys. The words, "Pharisees" and "woe" occur in the same verse six times in the Gospel of Matthew. Not good for the Pharisees. You really don't want Jesus saying "woe" to you. Throughout Scripture we see a poor correlation between those that are "successful" in the eyes of the world and those Jesus "hung out with."

See Mark 12:41-44, "The Widow's Offering." Jesus' heart was drawn to the poor widow's heart, not the rich people with their sizable donations. We might believe that older, more mature people deserve our attention rather than their youngsters. I think our Lord might disagree. The kids, many times, may be the smarter investment. Let's look at Matthew 18:2-4 (emphasis added), "He called a little child to him, and placed the child among them. And he said: "Truly I tell you, unless you change and become like little children, you will never enter the kingdom of heaven. Therefore, *whoever takes the lowly position of this child* is the greatest in the kingdom of heaven." If we are to be lowly, certainly we can treat others, whoever they are, in a respectful way. Also, check out Philippians 2:3-4 (emphasis added), "Do nothing out of selfish ambition or vain conceit. Rather, in humility *value others above yourselves*, not looking to your own interests but each of you to the interests of the others." Another way to douse the flames on arrogance or, perhaps, our natural or human tendencies to lift ourselves up (rather than others) is to recall Jesus' words in Matthew chapter 5, the beginning of "The Sermon of the Mount" and "The Beatitudes": poor in spirit, meek, hungry and thirsty for righteousness, merciful, and pure in heart. How can we be any of those things if we harbor racist thoughts?

And of course, Paul writes a wonderful conclusion to the subject in Galatians, chapter 3 verse 28: "There is neither Jew nor Gentile, neither slave nor free, nor is there male and female, for you are all one in Christ Jesus."

Pretty simple.

Prayer Points

"Prayer is not simply getting things from God, that is an initial form of prayer; prayer is getting into perfect communion with God."
—Oswald Chambers[85]

"There is not in the world a kind of life more sweet and delightful than that of a continual conversation with God."
—Brother Lawrence[86]

From one perspective, there seems to be two kinds of prayer. Perhaps one we can call "lunchtime" prayers, and the other a "continual conversation." A friend of mine suggested this wasn't even "prayer." It was an "awareness." Lunchtime prayer is targeted: perhaps thanking the Lord for the hamburger with triple cheese, double bacon, and a good portion of mayo. This type of prayer should also include a request that the Lord allows our systems to process the meal with no immediate or future damage. Additionally, a request for the strength and wisdom to enjoy a salad for dinner seems like a good idea. Continual prayer flows from the heart unabated, twenty-four hours each day (at least when we are not on the phone or trying to answer someone's question). It is the "default" position—what we fall back on when our daily activities are put on pause. The apostle Paul tells us in 1 Thessalonians 5 verse 17 to "pray continually." In fact, that is the entire verse, obviously making it one of the shortest verses in the Bible. Scripture is God-breathed. Verse and chapter divisions are not. Also consider Isaiah 26:3, "You will keep in perfect peace those whose minds are steadfast, because they

85   Chambers, O. (2017). *My Utmost for His Highest: Classic Edition* (3rd ed.). Our Daily Bread Publishing.

86   Herman, N. (1692). *The practice of the presence of God.* Christian Classics Ethereal Library. https://www.ccel.org/ccel/l/lawrence/practice/cache/practice.pdf.

trust in you." Steadfast minds abide and are relentless and focused. The ESV may do a better job helping us understand the original, "You keep him in perfect peace whose mind is *stayed on you*, because he trusts in you" (emphasis added). Continual prayer never includes the word "amen."

You are likely familiar with the acrostic A.C.T.S. This suggests, if not a literal structure or orderly movement through our prayers, certainly a heart condition. Adoration. Confession. Thanksgiving. Supplication. The Ligonier Ministries website contains an excellent, brief article on this acrostic. For our purposes, allow me to suggest that one of our biggest obstacles in prayer (but also that we mistakenly maintain in our life direction) is the focus on Supplication. Supplication is essentially *Gimme*, a common hurdle for us all. But ACTG is difficult, if not impossible, to pronounce. So, I "fix" the problem by putting the G in front of the ACT, which, of course, *is* the problem. We easily slip into the mode of asking for various things, whatever they may be, at the "expense" of the outpouring of our love and affection to our Lord. Let's agree that ACTG should always, each day—no matter what has landed in our laps—be the correct order. Our heart condition should be such that we deprioritize asking for stuff.

Broadly speaking, there seems to be three answers to prayer: yes, no, and the silent ceiling. We love "yes." But we tend to pray puny prayers. Let's use dinner, what we eat, as a metaphor. We often pray, "Dear Lord. I would like a burger from a fast-food restaurant." There's that burger again. If the Lord says yes, that is certainly not in our best interest. The other broad alternative, no, to our prayer request in this instance is clearly a better answer. We don't like no, but we must be convinced that God always chooses what is best for us. Period. Now, the third general response to our request: the silent ceiling.

What's up with that? God always answers prayer. How come I don't "hear" the answer? I am not sure what to do next. I am lost.

Back to the common struggle. Too many of us participate in the rusty-antenna malady. RAM? If sin is put away, you are being obedient, love the Lord with all your heart, and don't have a rusty antenna. You are just looking for the answer in the wrong place and/or at the wrong time. Silent ceiling then means "wait." Most of the time, "wait," is actually the best answer. It is the Lord telling us that He has a better plan. Back to the dinner metaphor. He is saying, "Hey, instead of sending you to a fast-food restaurant, I am planning to prepare for you a healthy, gourmet meal." And each one of us knows planning, gathering the ingredients, and cooking a multi-course healthy, gourmet meal takes a lot longer than swinging by the fast-food joint. And, for sure, it is better for us in many ways.

But, also, consider that if you love the Lord with *all* your heart and are truly yielded to Him, the silent ceiling may also mean, "You choose. I will bless You in whatever You do." The obvious question then becomes, "Okay, so, green light or red light?" Let there be no airspace between you and the Lord. Honestly seek to walk His path. It's not what you do, it's *why* you do it that matters. If that is your heart condition, you are automatically on the right path. Whatever you choose.

I'd love to tell you, dear reader, that when I get the silent ceiling, I simply smile, knowing full well the Lord has a better plan for me, and I go on my way. Well, sometimes I do that, but more than once I have been caught asking for a "second opinion." Why? If you can tell me, please, let me know. But I think I know the answer.

Something else to consider when we get a bit frustrated when offering simple, heartfelt prayers and the answer (or lack of answer) confuses us: It's not all about me.

Wow.

We often forget that simple line. We ask for stuff based on our sliver of existence. God is up there sustaining, choreographing, and empowering absolutely everything. We see the smallest part and, of course, from our narrow perspective. I think we can legitimately use the word "myopic." How about selfish? Simply remembering that life in every situation is very much more complicated should make it easier to understand the "apparent" delays. It's not all about us.

One more thought: Seems to me—and I may be wrong—that *specific* prayer carries more "weight" and is more potent as compared to the more generalized versions. If so, why? Not sure.

Maybe this requires us, the people involved, or those we are lifting up to be more honest, more open, and more vulnerable. Sharing specific needs or prayer requests forces a participation that casual requests do not.

Running Away from Falsehood and Lies

"Do not conform to the pattern of this world, but be transformed by the renewing of your mind. Then you will be able to test and approve what God's will is—his good, pleasing and perfect will."
—The Apostle Paul[87]

"God puts conforming to the lies of the world and renewing your mind to the truth in stark contrast."
— Craig Denison[88]

But some readers may protest, "How the heck are we as Christians to participate in or even influence various fields, such as Public Education and Politics? Given the current disregard of common rules and common sense, is not all lost?"

Great questions.

In future writing, I will attempt to convey a summarized version of the current debate on Climate Change. Bet you weren't expecting that. For now, please allow me to use the topic as an illustration only. Misinformation and a general breakdown in rational thinking have taken over the conversation. My undergraduate degree is in Environmental Sciences. I have a Master's in Geology and have worked in the Petroleum Industry for thirty-four years. I definitely do not qualify as an expert on the subject of Global Warming (now Climate Change), but I suspect I know more than most. In fact, my plans are to write a book on Climate Change—either the best idea I have had in a while or the worst. I can't tell from here. What intrigues me is how quickly people have fallen for and absorbed blatant disinformation and

87   Romans 12:2

88   Denison, C. (2020, Sept. 18). The renewal of your mind. *First15*. Retrieved March 17, 2021 from https://www.first15.org/09/18/the-renewal-of-your-mind/.

phony surficial positioning from both sides of the argument. This is my point. If a major portion of the public easily sides with the world system or the best marketed or loudest sales pitch, then preaching the gospel message and claiming the non-negotiable truth of the faith—in 180-degree contrast—will necessarily result in a roadblock. Accessing the foundational truths contained within basic apologetics becomes difficult. Scripture is truth. From cover to cover, the Bible mentions truth. Indeed, Jesus claimed to be truth, not just simply to tell the truth. Two different things. "Jesus answered, 'I am the way and the truth and the life. No one comes to the Father except through me'" (John 14:6).

Those with a propensity to live comfortably in the dark cannot see (recognize) the light. The danger is not the economic cost of implementing restrictions on burning fossil fuels, for instance. The danger is the focus and immersion in a wildly distorted reality at the expense of truth. I am doing the best I can to see or understand the "science" (or "perceived" science) in the much more important spiritual context. This is what we find ourselves up against every day in our attempt to influence the world for Him.

The argument above does not consider the illumination offered by the Holy Spirit. Accepting the truths of the Christian faith has never come naturally to anyone, regardless of our abilities. But God's help is vital to all understanding. All understanding—not just biblical. A significant cause of losing the ability to discern what is true stems from an individual or cultural decision to reject God. When God "leaves" (see 1 Sam. 4:21) as He often does when asked to leave, He takes His "gifts" with Him. James puts it this way in chapter 1 verse 17: "Every good and perfect gift is from above, coming down from the Father of the heavenly lights, who does not change like shifting shadows." King David tells us in Psalm 16:2, "I say to the LORD, 'You are my Lord; apart from you I have no good thing.'" Love is a choice, and God respects our choice to toss Him to the curb. If that is what we decide, then our ability to understand truth evaporates. Unfortunately, we see this too often, as relayed to us by the media here in the States.

I suggest the path forward is simply knowing we are to live immersed in truth—not just in the spiritual context, but in all ways. The world around us is drowning in lies and falsehood. This should not surprise us. The Holy Spirit helps us discern what is a lie. Recall Agur's request, "Keep falsehood and lies far from me" (Prov. 30:8). The immediate context most likely is a request to help him never be guilty of lying or believing and pronouncing falsehoods. It is possible to suggest that the Lord will "nip it in the bud" and not allow the deceptions to take root in the believer. The Holy Spirit will tap the Christian on the shoulder and gently tell us, "Don't go there," but, most of the time, will not disclose or explain what is actually occurring. This would take forever, and it is God's job to deal with, not ours.

Christ has defeated Satan, and God alone is sovereign. However, Satan continues to influence the world, especially in the arena of spiritual understanding. See 1 John 5:19. "We know that we are children of God, and that the whole world is under the control of the evil one." And 2 Corinthians 4:4, "The god of this age has blinded the minds of unbelievers, so that they cannot see the light of the gospel that displays the glory of Christ, who is the image of God." And we know that Satan is the father of lies, as in John 8:44: "You belong to your father, the devil, and you want to carry out your father's desires. He was a murderer from the beginning, not holding to the truth, for there is no truth in him. When he lies, he speaks his native language, for he is a liar and the father of lies." Again, we should not be surprised when hearing the news (in its various forms) that a good portion is most likely heavily distorted.

The question remains as to how we push back or influence in a positive way this degradation. I can only tell you how I deal with the problem. Can I expect to play even a minor role in putting the world back on track or delaying the inevitable? Of course not. What I have prayerfully chosen to do is watch current events unfold in light of eschatological considerations. Is it time for us to be discouraged? Should we give up? Certainly not. We should be encouraged, knowing that this is an exciting hour and God has chosen us to influence the people of the world when the time to do so is waning.

In general, I believe the proper way to view the end times is not to fret or desire to slow the process but simply to convey *urgency*. Similarly, a primary motivation to sharing our faith with those individuals around us should be the topic of urgency. Neither we—nor they—know how much time is left on the clock to accept the gift Christ offers. The culture—the world—is also on a clock. We know that the Anti-Christ spirit will be moving ahead swiftly over time. Put another way, the world system (that which opposes the Lord) will be taking greater control of the world's systems (governments, universities, entertainment, the mainstream media, and so on). More importantly, nothing on the calendar will ever pinpoint the rapture of the true church and the return of Christ. What we do know is that those events are approaching, and the end times and the prophecies will play out.

You Are What You Eat

"Doubt is not always a sign that a man is wrong; it may be a sign that he is thinking."
—Oswald Chambers[89]

One of the financial publishers I have subscribed to periodically puts out a terrific newsletter. My primary interest in his articles went past his comments on the world economy and geopolitics. In fact, there were often perspectives that he developed that I didn't follow or agree with. What I enjoyed most were his clearly *original* thoughts. This guy would come up with ideas that I heard nowhere else. That intrigued me.

When was the last time you (or I) had an original thought? I probably know the answer. It has been a while. A long while. One of the most common (and detrimental) behaviors of the human condition is that we often imitate mirrors. We all too quickly simply reflect what we have heard or read. Nothing more. When asked our opinion on something, there is little analysis or critical thinking applied. We simply regurgitate the input received from our favorite news channel, social media platform, text, email, or what have you. We are parrots. And, because we are all prone to recency bias, it is even a bit more troubling. We parrot mostly the stuff we *just* heard, forgetting what we heard and repeated in the past which may very well be inconsistent or possibly contradictory to what we say now. Investors know this too well in a broader context. Many of us believe the market will continue going up (if it has been going up) or continue going down (if it has "recently" been going down). Again, a common ailment we all share.

If we're immersed in something constantly, it eventually leaves a stain on us. As an example, even if seemingly benign,

89 Chambers, O. (2008). *The Quotable Oswald Chambers* (David McCasland, Ed.). Discovery House Publishing.

let us consider television commercials for medications. Have you seriously listened to what we are told, four times an hour, hour after hour, day after day?

"If you are allergic to Isavuconazonium, don't take it."
Oh, okay.

"For symptoms of a heart attack or stroke, get help right away."
Good idea.

How about the recordings at all our doctors' offices?

"If you are having an emergency, hang up and dial 911."
Thank you.

In a way, this stuff is hilarious. In another way (what I am speaking to today), it is not. Immersed in the silliness, we become, uh. . . silly—making it more difficult to adequately process what is vital.

How about this ad on the TV?

"Are you drowning in debt? It's not your fault."

Well, then whose fault is it? No, I am not heartless and do understand many people can lose a job, have medical bills roll in, and the car expire all at the same time. Sure, I get it. But that's not the target audience or the intent of the message (the sales pitch).

Fox News is quite capable (intended or not) of joining the crowd and becoming part of the problem. If I recall, between programs they run the comment, "Every story every fifteen minutes!"

What? Okay, I got it already.

"Breaking news!"

Breaking? You guys have been covering this story for weeks.

The same stuff, when repeated ad nauseam, can easily and quickly turn us into echo chambers. I can't believe I used that term. But it's true. Better term? Robots. Better still? Brainwashed.

As with many difficulties, the remedy is obvious. First, acknowledge the illness, which is many times the human condition. This is just what we do—who we are. Second, stop consuming the poison. Will Rogers is quoted as saying, "When you find yourself in a hole, quit digging".[90] Third, see the right

90   Young, R. (n.d.). *Will Rogers Legacy: Remembering That Old Cowboy*. ca.gov. https://www.parks.ca.gov/?page_id=23998

doctor (the Lord, of course). So, this is the plan: If we are going to parrot, it is best to parrot Scripture. As in Romans 12:2, "Do not conform to the pattern of this world, but be transformed by the renewing of your mind. Then you will be able to test and approve what God's will is—his good, pleasing and perfect will."

If we are what we eat, how about Scripture for dinner? Like Jeremiah: "When your words came, I ate them; they were my joy and my heart's delight, for I bear your name, LORD God Almighty" (Jer. 15:16).

Anybody Have a
Bible Handy?

"We fail in our duty to study God's Word not so much because it is difficult to understand, not so much because it is dull and boring, but because it is work. Our problem is not a lack of intelligence or a lack of passion. Our problem is that we are lazy."
—R.C. Sproul[91]

"If you wish to know God you must know his word; if you wish to perceive his power you must see how he worketh by his word; if you wish to know his purpose before it is actually brought to pass you can only discover it by his word."
—Charles Spurgeon[92]

A few years ago—well actually, a couple decades ago—I was invited to give a presentation to a Sunday school class at a mainline, denominational church north of Dallas. On the agenda was a brief look at the apparent contradiction between what we read in the Bible and our scientific theories or understanding pertaining to creation. If there truly was a conflict, which way should the Christian lean and why? How was I able to resolve being a Christian who takes the Bible "literally" and being a geoscientist? No plans to get into the topic now. At least not yet. Stay tuned.

I was at the point of describing Noah's Flood and wanted to make the suggestion that, being a world event which some people argue of catastrophic proportions, that the resultant

91   Sproul, R.C. (1977). *Knowing Scripture.* InterVarsity Press.

92   Spurgeon, C. (1881). *The Swiftly Running Word.* The Spurgeon Center for Biblical Preaching at Midwestern Seminary. https://www.spurgeon.org/resource-library/sermons/the-swiftly-running-word/#flipbook/.

sedimentary strata or evidence would be significant. But first we wanted to see what the Bible had to say, so, I said, "Let's take a look at Genesis chapter 7. Would someone read for us verses 17 through 20?" An uncomfortable silence came upon the group. There were about fifteen people in attendance. No one had a Bible! This was a Sunday school class, and nobody brought a Bible? No fear. The gentleman who obviously was "in charge" jumped up from his chair and dove into the cabinets with the full intent of finding the stash of hidden Bibles. Perhaps they would be a bit dusty, but we could handle that. Nothing. There were some back-and-forth glances, body-language apologies, a few shoulder shrugs, and then back to business. I read verses 17 through 20.

I hate to admit this to my readers, but there was a part of me, hopefully a hidden part, that enjoyed the panic. Forgive me. I actually considered just standing there with a disturbed expression on my face which meant, "I'm not in a rush. I am sure you can find a Bible somewhere in the church. Perhaps someone brought one to the Praise and Worship service in the main sanctuary?"

But I didn't. Oh, I *really* wanted to.

And, honestly, it was not particularly entertaining or funny. There were fifteen people present and all sorts of bookshelves and cabinets in the Sunday school classroom, but not one Bible! What did they talk about when we weren't discussing the topic of creation? Social Justice? Diversity? Progressivism? Travel plans? Golf?

When I led a Bible Study at work, I made sure we studied the Bible. Seemed like a reasonable thing to do. We wanted to know Jesus Christ. The *biblical* Jesus. I think you need a Bible to do that.

That Person Has Been with Jesus

"Trying harder to do better is imprinted on our cultural DNA. Self-reliance explains much of the material success of our society. But self-sufficiency is spiritual suicide."
—Jim Denison[93]

If we are to carry the Lord with us front and center throughout our lives, co-laboring with Christ and representing Him to those we see, and (more importantly) to those who see us, we will have to die to self each day. What we want people to see is Him, not us. Can we legitimately expect those on our path to say, "Hey, that person has been with Jesus"? Initially, we may view this thought with subtle amusement. We could quite easily chuckle under our breath, "Sure. I am going to remind someone of Jesus." Well, remember, the Christian is indwelt or is the temple of the Holy Spirit. Consider 1 Corinthians 6:19-20, "Do you not know that your bodies are temples of the Holy Spirit, who is in you, whom you have received from God? You are not your own; you were bought at a price. Therefore honor God with your bodies." The Holy Spirit is the very essence of Christ. Consider also that we are a priesthood: "But you are a chosen people, a royal priesthood, a holy nation, God's special possession, that you may declare the praises of him who called you out of darkness into his wonderful light" (1 Peter 2:9). So, is it possible to reflect Him to those around us? Absolutely.

How difficult is it to live the Christian lifestyle? Periodically, I would pose this question to the Bible Study. After about a twenty-minute open comment period, I would play the typical killjoy

93 Denison, J. (2019, Dec. 20). 'Star wars' and the 12 steps of the 'hero's journey': Finding god in surprising places. *Denison Forum*. Retrieved March 17, 2021 from https://www.denisonforum.org/columns/daily-article/star-wars-and-the-12-steps-of-the-heros-journey-finding-god-in-surprising-places/.

by calling time out and suggesting that the question had a trap door. Difficult? It is not *difficult*. It is impossible. As stated above, our only chance of living a life that will confuse (meant in a good way) those around us is to be immersed in the Spirit. Put in other words, die to self—constantly. When "we" are dead, then there is no one left but the Spirit in us to come to the surface.

Occasionally, when the alarm goes off, my first prayer of the day has gone something like this: "Lord, I'm gonna stay in bed this morning. You get up." Before you accuse me of being lazy or wanting to roll-over and feed Abbey (my black Lab) breakfast an hour later, the purpose of the prayer was to make a commitment: dedicating the day, no matter what happens, to the Lord. The mindset being, "Lord, let people see and hear *You* today. Not me." What do we have to offer those around us if we are driven by the natural man? Not much. It would be a far more profitable day if those we come across get a view of Christ.

The Package Deal

"God doesn't call us to something only to leave us to fend for ourselves. He is with us, he provides for us, and he enables us to finish the assignment."
—Stacy Reaoch[94]

It is too easy to overthink things, especially big, important things. Going to college. Trying to find a job. We often doubt ourselves and end up worrying about items we have no business worrying about. In fact, worrying in general is a mistake. As Jesus says, "Therefore do not worry about tomorrow, for tomorrow will worry about itself. Each day has enough trouble of its own" (Matt. 6:34). And possibly everybody's favorite in this regard, "Do not be anxious about anything, but in every situation, by prayer and petition, with thanksgiving, present your requests to God" (Phil. 4:6).

How am I going to accomplish all that I have to do? Emphasis is on the I (the me) which is the obvious blunder. Bottom line? You'll probably blow it. So what?

Here's my point. *If the Lord wants you to go to Nineveh, He will find you a camel.* If He wants you to attend Dallas Baptist University (DBU), its admissions office will accept your application. What we often do next is freak out, wondering how we are going to pay for it. *Don't know.* What I do know is, if God truly wants you to go to DBU, He will provide a way for "you" to pay for it. We make this stuff way too hard.

The Lord is into what I call "Package Deals." If He wants you to go to Disneyworld, He will provide park and airline tickets, taxi to and from the hotel, cash for food—you get it. Now, some people will and have challenged me at this point with this comment: "Tony, are you saying we just sit in our office and wait

94   Reaoch, S. (2018, Jan. 27). If he calls you, he will equip you. *The Gospel Coalition.* Retrieved March 17, 2021 from https://www.thegospelcoalition.org/article/if-he-calls-you-he-will-equip-you/.

for the phone to ring?" You know, I have heard this more than once, and, even as I type the challenge, I smile. *No.* We don't just sit on our can and wait.

Wait. Sometimes we are called to wait! Psalm 27:14 makes this clear. "Wait for the LORD; be strong and take heart and wait for the LORD." But that is not what we are talking about. What we are talking about is God's call. It is complete. You will have access to: finances, knowledge, physical strength, wisdom, time, focus. You see where I am going? Whatever God calls you to do, you will have what you need to not only do it but do it well. Incredibly well.

Okay, time for another challenge; "Tony, are you saying everything the Lord wants us to do will turn to gold?" *No.* Some of the stuff we do we simply do because we know He wants us to do it. I think the keyword here is "obedience." But, newsflash, it may not turn out the way we envisioned or hoped for. The Lord wasn't surprised, but we were. We had the wrong vision in our heads. So what?

Where is Your Jesus?

"Saddle up your horses. We've got a trail to blaze."
—Steven Curtis Chapman[95]

"God must do everything for us. Our part is to yield and trust."
— A.W. Tozer[96]

After I wrote this brief essay and put my initials in place (usually the last thing I do), I decided to do a Google search on the "Lord being our Navigator." *Good grief.* After reading three or four very well written and thought-out articles, I came seconds away from deleting what I had just written. Compared to the online articles written by pastors and Bible students, my contribution didn't strike me as being quite as "breathtaking" as I may have hoped. But a brief sigh and short prayer later, I decided to add this paragraph instead. In fact, what I am doing in this book is just tossing ideas your way, most of them definitely being biblical (CBC) and some of them just being *Carvalhoisms.* This is my way of putting a descriptor on thoughts that hopefully (1) have some meaning and some value and (2) may instigate further thought, prayer, and study. But go for it. Search "Jesus is my Navigator." Have fun. Below, just one more very light (smile) essay:

We frequently hear people saying, "Jesus is my Navigator." I assume that means they have given the map they travel to the Lord and understand that He should direct their paths, as in Psalm 119:35. "Direct me in the path of your commands, for there I find delight," and Proverbs 4:11, "I instruct you in the way of wisdom and lead you along straight paths."

95   Chapman, S., & Moore, G. (1992). The Great Adventure [Song]. On *The Great Adventure*. Bertelsmann Music Group.

96   Tozer, A.W. (2005). *The Pursuit of God.* Authentic Media (Original work published 1948).

Let's use the car metaphor. If He is the navigator, that puts Him in the front passenger seat.

Good. Maybe. . .

That's certainly a better place than the back seat. Is He your back-seat driver?

Uh-oh.

Some of us put Jesus in the trunk. In fact, when we hit a deep pothole, the trunk lid pops open, and guess what? Our Lord may no longer even be in the car. And we just tool down the highway. Sound familiar?

Remedy? Let Jesus *drive*. Daily, we should die to self, allowing the Holy Spirit to dominate. For today, let's just say we'll allow Jesus to drive—not navigate, but drive. Each time you reach for the steering wheel, pull back. Yield to Him. We belong to Him.

Do we still have free will? Absolutely. We can jump out of the car at any moment. I don't suggest doing that. Choose to *follow* Him. And wherever he pulls over and lets us out to accomplish what He wants us to do, be obedient and blossom. Paradise or desert. So what?

Who Are You?

"A surveyor spoke to hundreds of people at a busy intersection, asking each the question, 'Who are you?' Each person responded with what he or she did for a living: 'I'm a doctor' or 'I'm a teacher' or 'I'm a pastor.'"
—Jim Denison[97]

You want to have fun with people? Ask them who they are. Be serious. It's great conversation and, obviously, tells you a lot about the person you are speaking with. As Jim Denison tells us above, most people will automatically fall into the default, career-description position. That's usually when I do the Cramer (*Mad Money*) thing, pounding the "wrong" button. My body language says, "Try again." Next try usually is directed toward their family ties. My response?

"Better."

Better also means wrong. I am having too much fun.

"Try again. I am not going anywhere," I ask.

At this point, knowing something about me, they might choose the church they attend or their denomination. "I am a Methodist."

This is good. They are getting warmer. But warmer also means wrong.

The ever-increasing grin on my face usually keeps the reluctant contestant hopeful of arriving at the final destination. At this point I may say, "Okay. One more try before the clock runs out." Again, the body language, a casual lean forward perhaps, suggests, "I believe in you. Almost there. *Almost* there."

"I am a Christian."

Bingo! They won.

They don't win much, except a sigh of relief and the

97   Denison, J. (2017, Sept. 4). Three reasons to work: A labor day reflection. *Denison Forum*. Retrieved March 17, 2021 from https://www.denisonforum.org/columns/daily-article/three-reasons-work-labor-day-reflection/.

opportunity to talk about something else or order another blueberry muffin. But: success! This is where the game show host gets to tease them some more, suggesting we agree to add a bit of pizazz to their answer. Let's make it somewhat more intriguing or descriptive. How about, "I am the Hands and Feet of Jesus." "I am a Representative of the Kingdom." Or my favorite, "I am an Ambassador for Christ." As Paul writes in 2 Corinthians 5:20, "We are therefore Christ's ambassadors, as though God were making his appeal through us. We implore you on Christ's behalf: Be reconciled to God."

There is nothing, dear reader, more important.

You see how meaningful this is. If people don't understand the question or you just talked about their wife and kids (for instance), you get a legitimate flag thrown on the field. If you are meeting with your Christian buddies, they are fair game. Who are you? At the top of our beanies—the first thing out of mouth—the obvious answer is (should be), "I am a Christian." That is who we are. All those other things, being a geologist (*oh dear*), a husband, wife, dad, or mom are, of course, vitally important and wonderful blessings, but compared to our relationship to Christ?

Check out Matthew 10:37. "Anyone who loves their father or mother more than me is not worthy of me; anyone who loves their son or daughter more than me is not worthy of me."

You Know What God Should Do?

Lord I give my life.
A living sacrifice.
To reach a world in need.
To be your hands and feet.
—Casting Crowns[98]

"God has given you a Kingdom assignment he has given to
no one else."
—Jim Denison[99]

Don't you really like telling God what He should do? Doesn't that sound like a brilliant maneuver? What God should do when someone accepts Christ as their personal Lord and Savior—when they are reborn and no longer residents of planet earth but the tabernacle in heaven?

THE LORD: "Hey, lightning bolt. Busy?"

THE LIGHTNING BOLT: "No, Sir."

THE LORD: "See that guy down there?"

THE LIGHTNING BOLT: "The one with the smile on his face? The guy that looks a lot like your Son?"

THE LORD: "Yes, him. He's been having a rough time. Just lost his job. Sure, he is still smiling. That's great. He gets it.

98   Hall, M. (2005). Lifesong [Song]. On *Lifesong*. Warner Chappell Music.

99   Denison, J. (2017, Dec. 11). Why you weren't invited to the 'Star Wars' premiere. *Denison Forum*. Retrieved March 17, 2021 from https://www.denisonforum.org/columns/daily-article/werent-invited-star-wars-premiere/.

But, since he now lives here with us, the next time he walks out to his car, I would like you to weld him to the pavement. Doesn't need to be raining or even cloudy. In fact," THE LORD says with a smile, "I am thinking a lightning bolt on a day with a perfectly blue sky—that may actually get a lot of peoples' attention."

THE LIGHTNING BOLT: "On my way. This will be fun."

That's what God should do. But He doesn't. Why not? This isn't a trick question. This is pretty easy.

I have said this before and will again and again and again. *Christians are in full-time ministry, whether we know it or not.* The primary (well, essentially the only) reason we are left here after we truly accept the gift offered to us by Jesus is to *represent* Him to a lost world. We are His hands and feet. We are his ambassadors. The Holy Spirit resides in us. Consider what Paul writes here,

> All this is from God, who reconciled us to himself through Christ and gave us the ministry of reconciliation: that God was reconciling the world to himself in Christ, not counting people's sins against them. And he has committed to us the message of reconciliation. We are therefore Christ's ambassadors, as though God were making his appeal through us. We implore you on Christ's behalf: Be reconciled to God. (2 Cor. 5:18-20)

Dear reader, please, don't put this book down until that sinks in as deeply as possible and takes hold of you. These are exciting times. You were put here and are now left here to make eternal differences that, in fact, only you can do. There is no other *you*.

Something else to remember is that we work for a "company" that has a worldwide presence, has been in business for two thousand years, and can't go bankrupt. The top person in the company owns everything. In fact, the greatest job on earth is being a Christian. What would you trade it for? We report to the King of the Universe. I fear we don't contemplate this life-changing truth as often as we should. A daily dose would be terrific medicine for any ailment.

If you are truly born again, you have a job to do. Everything else is simply the means to an end. The end is patiently persuading (reasoning) and living in such a way (attracting) as many people as possible, so that they make it to the right side of eternity with us.

Five Questions with No Easy Answers

1. Why are there not Bibles in every language spoken in the world?

2. Why are there not more Pregnancy Medical Clinics (PMCs), formerly known as Pregnancy Resource Centers (PRCs), equipped with 3D or 4D ultrasounds in the U.S.?

3. Why are there not Bible studies in every place of employment in the U.S.?

4. Why are there not more Christians who tithe?

5. Why are there not more people in the U.S. that tolerate Christians and Jews? We tolerate everyone else.

About the Author

Tony Carvalho recently retired to the Florida Panhandle after working in the petroleum industry in Texas and Oklahoma for over thirty years. His last position was SVP at Chief Oil & Gas, but he preferred to be known as the Bible Study Guy. Chief participated in the early development of horizontal drilling, fracking, and the natural gas and oil shale revolution. He had a front row seat to the Lord putting the right people in the right place at the right time leading to a major change in the world geopolitical arena. While he was at Chief, the company closed 7 sales in 7 years for 7 billion dollars. He enjoys making the case for the full integration of faith and work and encouraging believers to expect great things as they look up and dedicate all areas of their lives to their Lord and Savior Jesus Christ. He is the founder of Lehigh Ministries.

Lehigh Ministries is currently engaged in various outreach activities, including an Oasis Effort designed to help reduce the rate of burnout in the minister, pastor, and missionary population.